TREASURE
YOURSELF

TREASURE
YOURSELF

Power Thoughts for My Generation

MIRANDA KERR

HAY HOUSE, INC.

Carlsbad, California • New York City
London • Sydney • Johannesburg
Vancouver • Hong Kong • New Delhi

Y O U

It is not that we don't have the strength within us . . .
We have more strength than we could possibly imagine.

Most of us fail to see it within ourselves
yet so willingly see it in others.

What if we nurtured ourselves to the point where
we discovered and experienced our own greatness?

What if we finally realized that we are limited
only by our thoughts and by what we think is or
isn't possible for us? After all, that is the truth . . .
nothing more, nothing less.

It is our thoughts that determine our experiences,
not only of ourselves, but of our world and of others . . .

Too often we fail to see that at any given moment we have a
choice to alter our lives, our existence.

Too often we are driven automatically by who we think we
are or should be as opposed to who we possibly could be . . .

Sometimes we choose to be angry, ungrateful, resentful,
and jealous when instead we have the ability to choose to
be accepting, forgiving, and grateful for all that we have . . .

Choose (*with goodness in your heart*) to be brave,
courageous, and adventurous in this world and
acknowledge all who are being just that, for they
have overcome what many have yet to overcome . . .
the fear of knowing who they really are.

Look forward and dream of what's possible for your life . . .
and remember that the only thing limiting
you is your thoughts.

Only you have the power to change your thoughts.
Alter your thoughts and you alter your world.

— *Miranda Kerr*

~~~~~~~

This book is dedicated to all of the amazing,
unique, and talented young women in this world.
Through this book and through your own journey
of self-discovery, may you come to see just
how incredible you really are.

CONTENTS

*I*t was the early blossoming of spring and a girl was wandering through a garden when she discovered a cocoon hanging from the branch of a tree. It was almost time for a butterfly to emerge. Fascinated with her discovery, she returned to the garden daily, enthusiastic to see all that would happen and hoping never to miss a thing.

One day a small opening appeared, and the girl saw the butterfly struggling to free itself from its cocoon and enter a new world. She watched intently—until the butterfly seemed to have stopped making progress. It appeared as if it had gone as far as possible and could go no further.

The girl made a sudden decision; she began to remove pieces of the cocoon that were obstructing the butterfly. Excited, she watched as the butterfly emerged, hoping its wings would unfold. But her excitement turned into dismay as the butterfly remained unable to move.

It was then that the girl realized what was happening: the cocoon was intended to create the struggle necessary for the butterfly to fly. In fact, it was not trying to escape . . . this was just nature's way of making its wings stronger. It occurred to the girl that the butterfly would actually be grateful to the cocoon for the struggle that they would share.

— Anonymous

Stories about nature and the way its creatures weather the storms remind me to appreciate all that is around me and be grateful for everything I have and all that is yet to unfold. I really love this particular story and it has a special meaning for me.

Sometimes I'm the girl—impatient, overexcited, and rushing in to fix things for myself and for others rather than letting events unfold naturally. Mostly I try to be the butterfly, though: calmly and bravely encountering life's challenges and becoming stronger along the way.

Life has thrown some rocks in my stream, but each one has helped me become stronger, more confident, and definitely more determined. I've come to realize that every challenge and obstacle—every rock I've found on my path—has helped make me the person I am today.

Thinking about things this way has helped me to accept difficult times and even welcome them as opportunities to grow. We are all that butterfly in the story, destined to emerge from the cocoon as incredible, gifted, and talented individuals. Our journeys are all unique; the colors on our wings are not the same, but at the end of the day we all have the same goal—to get out into the world and fly. If we didn't face obstacles on our journey, then we wouldn't evolve as individuals. I believe it is these challenges that make us stronger.

I am a huge believer in the power of positive thinking. We all have unlimited potential, and if we accept the obstacles that cross our paths and learn from the lessons involved, we can reach our full potential. This book is a compilation of the lessons I have learned so far, from personal experience, as well as a collection of the wisdom I have gleaned from others whom I admire and who have inspired me.

In reading this book, you will see I have used the analogy of women/girls being as unique and as individual as every flower. For example, a rose—although it is different from a lily—is still just as stunning. Likewise, a frangipani is just as unique and beautiful in its own right as an orchid.

Over the years I have been blessed to have amazing women contribute to my life. My mum, nan, aunties, Mrs. Middlebrook, friends, work colleagues—they've all played an integral part and have helped shape me or make my life more interesting in some way. Each of these women is totally unique and beautiful, like each and every flower. I have asked each of them to contribute to my book by drawing their favorite flower, as an acknowledgment of how special they are to me.

I have placed their drawings or illustrations throughout the chapters of this book. I ask you to join with me in sharing their uniqueness and love, and grant them the opportunity to share part of themselves with you. I love them and thank them for sharing my journey and contributing so positively to my life.

I honestly believe there is nothing stopping us from embracing our dreams and creating the lives we wish to live.

All it takes is a shift in the way we think. I love what Louise L. Hay says: "Every thought I think is creating my future."

It's so important to keep positive and say "Yes!" to life, I believe. I use positive affirmations as a way to help me achieve this sense of positivity, because certain sayings and words have empowered me in my life and have helped me to follow my dreams and reach my goals. Said every morning and every night—and even many times during the day— power thoughts can help you, too.

I wish to share my inspiration with you so that you will treasure and believe in yourself, have faith in your abilities, accept who you are, and uncover your own unique gifts. We all have wings, but it is up to each one of us to have the courage to fly. My hope is that these words and the affirmations included will help empower you to reach for your dreams even in difficult times. With action, anything in life is possible.

Sometimes, challenges and struggles are exactly what we need in our lives . . .

May you welcome every effort, every struggle, and every challenge and appreciate all your blessings . . . may you open your wings and fly!

— *Miranda Kerr*
    XXX

belinda

hannah

maja

miranda

life lessons

*What follows is a little about my life to help
you see how I got to where I am today.*

Country life... It all began for me in Gunnedah,
New South Wales—a small country town in rural
Australia. Gunnedah is a typical country town. Everyone
knows everyone and people are genuinely concerned about
each other. It's a beautiful little town and is surrounded
by nature and wide-open spaces. Like other country
towns, Gunnedah doesn't have huge department stores or
shopping malls.

I was raised by my parents and grew up with my wonderful, kind-hearted brother, Matthew; and my grandparents, cousins, aunts, and uncles were always around.

My childhood was blessed and I'm very grateful to have a family that showed me unconditional love, understanding, and acceptance. My parents taught me many valuable lessons about life, and I definitely wouldn't be where I am today without their continuous support.

My childhood was filled with fun, excitement, and adventure. My parents, my brother, and I lived in the town, but each day our grandmother picked up Matthew and me from school. We spent our time on our grandparents' farm with our cousins and the kids Nan used to babysit. We'd ride motorbikes and horses, drive the old cars in the paddock, build cubby houses, play dress-up, and climb trees. These are some of my fondest memories.

From an early age I played a lot of sports like basketball and netball, as well as doing gymnastics, and as I got older I also played touch football. I spent quite a bit of time hanging out with my friends, singing, painting, dancing, and having sleepovers at my place.

My life's path has taken me on an interesting and amazing journey. A friend secretly entered me in the 1997 *Dolly Magazine* CoverGirl competition, which is where my modeling career began. To win was such a surprise! It was a fantastic experience. Not long after, my family and I relocated to Brisbane, where I graduated from high school. I was reluctant to move to the city because I am a country girl at heart. I missed Gunnedah and, like anyone who moves away, I missed my friends. It was a big change. I was quite fortunate, though: from the first day at my new school I was welcomed by a great group of girls and made some lifelong friends. Things seemed to be going really well, until something happened that changed my life forever.

~~~~~~~

Overcoming obstacles... I'm sure you have had many experiences that have altered the way you think and feel about life. I want to share with you something that happened to me that was really significant, and at the time was one of the biggest challenges I had ever faced.

When I was 16, I was deeply in love with Chris, my first boyfriend. We had been dating for two years and I had just left Gunnedah and moved to Brisbane, when he was killed instantly in a car accident, and all of a sudden it felt as though my world had fallen apart. Although we were young, we had both dreamed of and talked about spending the rest of our lives together. I was devastated, and it felt like I had fallen into a dark hole, from which it took me a long time to surface. Being so young, it was difficult to imagine how things could ever get better and how the light I had felt in my life could shine again. I felt as if my heart had been ripped from my chest and I didn't know what to do.

Having grown up so close to nature in Gunnedah, however, I had learned from an early age that change is inevitable, though it can be painful; summer becomes autumn and winter turns to spring, life has a rhythm. I was also fortunate enough to have the love and understanding of my family and friends and time to heal.

Chris's death taught me that the people who touch your life are always with you. It taught me that I have the choice to be grateful for the time I had with him instead of dwelling on losing him, and it made me realize that life is so fragile that we need to really live and appreciate every moment. It also taught me that no one can heal your pain but yourself, and through the power of gratitude and acceptance I was able to move forward.

I now say to myself, "I trust the process of life" to remind me that even in the darkest hours, there is still light and possibility. I've learned not to take my family, my friends, or my life for granted. I try to live each day in a positive way and to make a difference wherever my path takes me.

~~~~~~~

Pursuing the dream... After graduating from high school, I moved to Sydney and began to pursue modeling as a career. I quickly became independent; although my parents were there for backup should I have needed them, from the time I moved to Sydney I basically supported myself and was accountable for my own finances. Modeling is a tough world to break into and, despite my earlier success in *Dolly*, like many other girls I faced a lot of rejection. It was tough, but every time I felt down or lost a job, I would use the affirmations I read in Louise L. Hay's books and say things to myself like, "I flow freely and lovingly with life" or "Life supports me." These affirmations really helped me along the way.

Fortunately, I always secured enough work to support myself . . . and even sometimes found myself working internationally. One time I was in Japan on a job, and the company I was working for were worried that I was too tan for the image they wanted to portray. It was then I began to realize that being rejected on the basis of how I looked was something I needed to come to terms with if I was to succeed in the modeling industry. I could either internalize it as meaning that something was wrong with me, or simply accept that at that moment in time I was not suited for the needs of that particular campaign or shoot. This experience really helped me realize that I can't please everyone all of the time. I decided then to stay true to myself and my principles. As I surrendered to this, my world opened up with many new and exciting possibilities.

~~~~~~~

Staying grounded... Coming from a small country town and being so connected to the earth helps me keep my feet on the ground. At first I couldn't imagine earning my living from modeling, and in those first few years I felt uncertain about modeling as a career. So in the early days of working I also studied psychology and nutrition. This helped me form my own ideas about health and wellness, which are so important to me today and have really helped to keep me grounded, healthy, and balanced.

~~~~~~~

Moving on... Essentially, I am an adventurous and driven person. I wanted a bigger challenge than I could find in Australia, so in 2005—at 22 years of age—when the opportunity presented itself to me, I moved to New York. This journey has changed my life in many ways and helped me discover more about myself; a continual process.

New York is a big city, and at first I lived in a house with other models, thinking this would be the most secure way to live. After a while I felt I needed more freedom and space, so I rented my own apartment and more recently purchased an apartment in Manhattan. I love having my own home. It's a sanctuary for me when I need some peace and time to recharge my batteries.

Being grounded and taking care of myself physically and spiritually is really important to me. I work hard so

I try to balance my life with meditation, chanting, and yoga. Being balanced also means spending time with great friends. I am so thankful for the friends I have; their constant love and support is something I appreciate. I love hanging out with them, my family, and of course Frankie, my little Yorkshire terrier.

I also find it wonderful to meet new people. Getting to know others is invaluable, as they can enrich and expand your view on life. This particular affirmation really sustains me: "I experience love wherever I go." It reminds me to seek balance and to try my best to live in the moment, enjoy every minute of life, and hope to somehow make a positive difference in the world.

~~~~~~~~

A world of opportunities… I believe I have been given an opportunity to do something useful and positive in the world. I had a great childhood filled with love and support, for which I am deeply grateful. I am very fortunate and life has been generous. However, like anyone, I have been through some challenging times and experiences that have tested my strength and resolve. Without these dark moments I wouldn't be the person I am today.

Success can easily transform you into someone you never intended to become, and that's why it's important to always take time out from life and think about what you are doing and your reasons for doing so. Challenges remind me of what is most important to me, such as my family and my friends. When I face a difficult decision I find that quiet space within and, rather than immediately tearing open the cocoon like the girl in the butterfly story, I reflect on what is important to me and what I'm here to do.

Overall, I believe wholeheartedly that gratitude is the key to success and to life in general. I try my best not to take all I've got for granted and greatly appreciate the opportunities that I have been given. I also appreciate the opportunity to reach you with this book . . . hopefully touching your life in some small way.

~~~~~~~

Loving yourself... Oscar Wilde said, "To love oneself is the beginning of a lifelong romance." I believe that loving and treasuring yourself is essential for happiness. It's about treasuring who you are as a person and accepting, respecting, and honoring yourself.

This is something I have struggled with personally. Loving yourself stems from the belief that "Who I am is enough" and that the qualities you possess are unique, worthwhile, and special. It is about being grateful for what you have been given, accepting who you are, and being compassionate toward yourself. It's like a beautiful reflection. What you see in yourself is what you see in everyone else around you.

In my eyes we are all equal. No one person is more special than another. In order to love others fully, you need to first love and accept yourself. You could spend your whole life wishing you were someone else and never really appreciate the person you actually are and the things that you have to offer. When you see yourself as a unique individual and understand that you are truly irreplaceable and that everyone is different and special just the way they are, you get the opportunity to really accept who you are and fully embrace yourself. That's when the magic of the universe radiateswithin us and automatically, without us even knowing, our inner joy, enthusiasm, and happiness is transferred to others.

One of the most important things I've realized is that we can all choose how to live our lives, no matter what the circumstances. You can choose how you feel when you get up in the morning. You can think, "Today is going to be pretty much the same as yesterday. I wish I could go back to sleep," or alternatively, "Today is going to be a wonderful day full of new and exciting experiences." Once you realize you can choose how you experience yourself, you start to open your world to unlimited possibilities and opportunities, and people are automatically drawn toward you and your enthusiasm.

~~~~~~~

Embracing challenges... Life in the world we live in can be pretty intense; we are constantly bombarded by information and noise. You could be in a busy city with all the hustle and bustle of millions of people, or in front of a computer screen, bombarded by trillions of different messages and opinions. It can be easy to become so caught up in just getting through the day that you forget to switch everything off sometimes and just listen to yourself. However, this is the way you stay strong and clear about who you are and what you really want in life.

I like to think that we are all unique flowers in the amazing garden we call Earth. No two of us are the same, nor should we ever want to be. We all have a place here. A daisy is as beautiful as a sunflower. We all face challenges in different ways, and we all have different strengths to help us through life. To find your strength, my advice would be to get to know who you are and listen to yourself before doing anything else. Think about your options and the consequences of each action you might take. Strive to be the best you can be and focus on who you are in each moment.

I believe the only way to handle a challenge is to face it head on with an open mind and heart. Like the butterfly in the story at the beginning of this book, challenges are what life gives us to make us stronger. Welcome challenges and you will open the doors to opportunity and growth. We might have huge hurdles that pop up now and then, but after we scale those heights and come back down on the other side there is always a great sense of achievement. Your own strength will be reflected back to you as you realize what you can accomplish. If you face those rocks in the stream with a positive attitude, things may not be as hard as you first thought. The rocks can become places to stop and take a breath, giving you the chance to really assess where you are. It's important during these challenging times to go within yourself and listen to your intuition.

When things seem at their worst or don't seem to be going to plan, instead of feeling down, start each day by saying to yourself: "How amazing it is to be alive! What a wondrous feeling I have inside! I am awake, healthy, and full of joy!" Visualize every cell in your body being filled with vitality, health, and love.

~~~~~~~~

Growth and change... I try to remind myself that with every hard time, whether it is a challenge that turns your life upside down or a simple occurrence that gets in the way of where you want to go, afterward there is *always* an act of creation. Like a forest that grows back after a fire, there are always new developments taking place. Life happens in cycles; most challenging moments in your life will pass, and a new phase of adventure will emerge.

The first part of change is generally the most confronting. More often than not we don't expect it, and that's when our sense of self gets tested. When this happens to me, instead of trying to immediately change my emotions, which can be jarring, I cocoon myself with things that make me feel better and try my best to sit with and accept how I feel. This doesn't mean that I dwell on things and immerse myself in misery . . . it just means that I give myself time to acknowledge how I am truly feeling.

When I am faced with troubles and filled with doubt, I am grateful for the strength it inspires within me. When nothing seems to go the way I want, I strive to maintain my composure and be grateful for the experience. When I let myself experience the feelings that I have, the discomfort passes faster than if I tried to push the feelings away. When I have truly experienced these feelings, my good sense and inner wisdom then have the opportunity to guide my words and actions rather than tension overwhelming me.

Once you have accepted your feelings about something, the next phase is a time in which you can use your imagination to think about what you want to happen next. When faced with a challenge, think of how success would feel, smell, taste, sound, and look. Pick out your colors, shapes, and textures and hold them in your mind. Nothing in your reality happens without your imagination, without it first being a thought. This is also the stage where you can focus on the "you" that you want to be as you shed the old skin. You might want to learn a different skill to face your challenge, develop more confidence, or even just experience new things in life. These are the things I think about when I am faced with a challenging situation or inevitable change.

~~~~~~~

Get ready to fly... When I have a clear picture of what I want, a transformation occurs. I feel empowered as my wings start taking shape and I feel ready to fly.

Action is what separates the dreamers from those who actually live out their dreams. At first you might be afraid to take the first step because you fear you might fail, but I think of failure as education—it gives you the knowledge you need to succeed.

When trying to achieve something, you might stumble along the way, but this is all part of the learning process. Just pick yourself up and try again. Like Henry Ford said, "Whether you think that you can or that you can't, you are usually right."

After all that hard work the next step is to prepare yourself to fly. Your crumpled, soggy wings are now dry, so you can expand them and make things happen! Enjoy and savor your success. Then whenever you face your next challenge reflect on that moment and remember what it felt like to get through it.

~~~~~~~~

Guidance from within... When I'm faced with a challenge, I seek guidance from within and surround myself with people who are loving and supportive. I'm an independent person by nature, and because of the amount of traveling alone I have done, it has been hard for me to accept that others can be there for me. I've now realized, through my challenges and through the support of my family and friends, that we never really have to be alone. My family is supportive, no matter how good or bad things are. Accepting that others in your life—friends, colleagues, and teachers—are willing to help if you would only ask is a true blessing.

Some of my biggest challenges have occurred when I've been on shoots. No matter how old you are there will always be elements of peer pressure around you. I remember one time I was on a shoot with a group of girls, and the photographer was encouraging everyone to go a little wild. I was shocked as to how far the girls were willing to go to impress the photographer and to show how sexy they could be.

They started throwing food at each other and rubbing it all over their bodies while starting to undress. It was in this moment I reminded myself that I am in control of my life: no one can dictate what I should or shouldn't do or how I should behave.

If you feel pressured, it's important to take a step back, breathe, and really think about your options and how the situation is making you feel. Ask yourself: "Is this who I really am, and am I being true to my values?" It doesn't matter what anyone else thinks. Your opinion of you is all that matters. In the situation that I found myself in, I realized I didn't need to partake in that kind of activity even though there was pressure to do so.

When I took a step back it helped keep me in the moment so that I could make the right choice for me. Knowing your own power, having your own opinions, and listening to your inner voice will mean that the decisions you make will be right for you. You decide how you think and feel about any situation, place, or person.

~~~~~~~

Getting Personal:
— What has been a big challenge for you?
— How did you cope with it?
— Who helped you to get through it?
— How would you cope with it now?

annette   *shonagh*   *gabby*

step out with confidence

annie

One of the key ingredients to having self-confidence is accepting and loving yourself: being comfortable in your own skin. If you want to have self-confidence then you must realize that accepting yourself and loving yourself go hand in hand. The more you learn about yourself the more you are able to offer compassion, not only to yourself but to others—and from compassion flows love. When you accept and appreciate yourself you can handle any situation with class, dignity, and respect.

Confidence is something that I have particularly struggled with, especially when I was younger. I remember when

I first started modeling, people on the shoot (make-up artists, photographers, etc.) would give me compliments, and I truly thought they were saying those things because they were just trying to make me feel good about myself. I wasn't embracing and accepting myself. I now realize that when people give me compliments I need to receive them wholeheartedly and accept them as the gift they are.

Sometimes others have the ability to see our inner and outer beauty when we fail to see it in ourselves.

~~~~~~~

Your authentic self... Trying to hold on to the authentic "you" can be a challenge in today's world. Exactly how we identify ourselves is becoming more and more of a priority. We are all familiar with social-media sites such as Facebook and Twitter that give us the opportunity to create an identity that we can show to the public. The amount of information that we can display about ourselves is virtually limitless, and it shows that the value we place on self-image is becoming increasingly apparent. But it's also important to remember not to lose who we are under the pressure to conform to social expectations of what's acceptable. Everyone has a need to fit in, and it can be really easy to sacrifice yourself for who you think you should be, instead of accepting who you really are.

The genuinely authentic people I know who are happy with where they are in life have a few things in common. They know their strengths and their weaknesses, and they *accept both*. Your authentic self doesn't have to be picture perfect for society's standards. Being the "real" and "authentic" *you* is all that counts.

~~~~~~~

Confidence is appealing... Modeling is a tough industry, and it's hard to say whether confidence can get you anywhere, but what I do know for sure is that the girls who have confidence and healthy habits enjoy themselves much more than those who don't. I find people who are honest with themselves and the people around them really appealing. A man or a woman who is confident in who they are—yet completely relaxed, humble, and down to earth—is extremely attractive. Knowing yourself and being real is the best way to be.

As you become more confident in yourself and your abilities, you can face rejection without it being devastating because you realize that it doesn't change who you are and what you bring to the world.

There will always be people who won't accept everything you do or stand for. What distinguishes someone who is confident from someone who is not is how he or she handles rejection. What is also good to remember is that the things others might not like about you could be the very things that make you different and unique. They could even be the values that you cherish! I keep reminding myself that rejection can sometimes be a blessing in disguise and the universe has something better in store for me. I try to look at it as simply another step toward my destiny.

~~~~~~~

Smile often... In my opinion a genuine smile is the most confident and attractive thing anyone can wear. Nothing is more beautiful than a smile that comes from the heart. A happy, confident person is charismatic and definitely more fun to be around and usually a lot more attractive. A smile radiates warmth from within. A smile says, "I'm confident and have a lot to offer the world."

~~~~~~~

Everything happens for a reason... I am a big believer that everything happens in life for a reason. I try to live in the moment and give my best at everything I do, and I trust that the right path will open before me.

Using positive affirmations keeps me open to change and helps me deal with self-doubt. Sometimes feeling doubtful about something can be a good wake-up call; a time to think carefully about what's really going on. Taking time to reflect on any doubts can be a useful process in which you look within to discover your true beliefs. There will always be challenges, obstacles and less-than-perfect situations, but if you take things step-by-step you will grow stronger and more confident in your own abilities.

There was a time in high school when I was being picked on by one of the girls in our year. This particular girl was always picking on someone and it was my turn. I remember being really scared of her, so I hated going to school. It got to the point where I didn't want to go to school at all. My parents had a long talk with me. They told me to stand up for what I thought was right; not to be rude, but to be honest with this girl, and tell her what effect she had on people and how terrible she made other people feel.

I remember going to school the next day, and sure enough, she said something mean to me. I was much smaller than she was, but as scared as I was I told her exactly what I thought. I told her things that no one else was willing or brave enough to tell her. I told her the only reason people hung around her was because they were scared of her and that she couldn't see they weren't really her friends. The ones she thought were her friends only pretended to be out of fear. She was hurt and cried. I didn't want to hurt her; I just wanted to tell her the truth, and I did. In doing so I stood up for myself and for others when I didn't think I could. It is interesting because after that I decided the situation with this girl happened for a reason, which was for me to learn to be stronger. As it turned out, my speaking up helped her—she stopped picking on people and got to know what it was like to have real friends, ones who really liked her. We ended up becoming friends and are friends to this day, and I am thankful for the process we went through together.

Knowing yourself and coming to trust your feelings and your intuition will open up your life to greater possibilities and keep you moving toward your goals. One thing I have learned is that we should trust our "gut" instincts. Ultimately, only **we** know what is best for us.

~~~~~~~~

Go for what you want… Some people are taught to believe that it's better to be silent than to rock the boat. But in my opinion, you are worse off if you remain silent, because you can find yourself squashing your own desires to accommodate others. We all worry at some point about the opinions of others, especially those whom we value. We stress ourselves out if we have to say "No" to someone we love, or we avoid saying anything if someone cuts in front of us or even speaks over us. But in the end, it's important for us to learn to value ourselves enough to stand up for what we know is right and for what we want, otherwise we will never get it.

~~~~~~~~

Being assertive... Assertiveness is a quality that enables you to endure the discomfort of doing what you believe is right even if you feel the emotional pressure that comes with going against the grain. There is a difference between being assertive and being aggressive, though. I've seen a lot of people who have come across as really dominating but believe they are just asserting their opinion. Being assertive doesn't mean that you always have to get your way . . . it just means you speak honestly and compassionately about your thoughts, beliefs, and opinions. There should be a balance in all things. It's important not to be too passive and let people take advantage of or use you; but, equally important, being too aggressive or even begrudging will not serve your highest good. By taking note of how you behave around other people, you can make a conscious effort to express how you feel in a harmonious way.

Self-doubt, however, is different. Self-doubt happens when you allow negative thoughts to stop you from moving forward and enjoying this wonderful life. These self-limiting beliefs can alter the way you behave—over-promoting yourself, being constantly defensive or even avoiding conversations and interactions with other people. This is the time when you can use some positive affirmations to challenge these thoughts. I like saying to myself, "I am awake, alive, and full of energy" and "I release any negative or fearful thoughts. I am safe."

Confidence is one of our greatest assets as individuals, and as we carry it within us, we can face any situation. Believing in our own capabilities also means knowing and having the means to rely on other sources for information and help if we cannot handle a situation completely on our own.

~~~~~~~~

Enjoy yourself... We are here to enjoy life and the experiences we have. We are here to make mistakes and sometimes look a little silly. I remember once in Milan, at one of my first fashion shows overseas, I was given shoes that were three sizes too big. When I realized and told my dresser, she just handed me a bunch of tissues as the show was about to start. I frantically stuffed the toes with as much tissue as possible and hoped for the best. I made it to the end of the runway, but as I turned around my left shoe went flying off into the crowd! I didn't know whether to laugh or cry so I decided to smile and keep walking with one shoe on and one foot on my tippy toes! It was at that moment I chose to see the funny side, and I think the crowd did, too.

We have the power to choose how we respond in any situation. Our ability to see the humor in those times can determine the quality of our response.

~~~~~~~

Getting Personal:
— What are you good at?
— What negative thoughts do you think most often?
— Can you turn these around by creating positive thoughts?
— How do you feel about yourself?
— Can you remember a time when you felt silly?
— How did you choose to react then?
— How would you react now?

jeanie   *ursula*   *tammy*   *amber*

red for passion

georgia

One of the most vital things you can do to increase your confidence and welcome challenge is to find your passion. With passion comes belief, determination, and a willingness to trust in your instincts. I believe that deep down we all know what we are passionate about. Sometimes we hide it behind the needs of others and deny what we truly feel inside.

I know many people who seemed to know what they wanted to do from an early age and now love the career they chose. Other people are on a search and may find themselves along many career paths before they stick to one that makes them happy. If you haven't found your passion yet, try not to get disheartened. Sometimes if you are going down a twisted path with lots of curves and bends, it still leads you to the exact place you need to be—it just takes a little longer. If you go down one career path and then change to another, all that knowledge can add depth to what you are doing now, making your set of skills more unique. There is no such thing as knowledge wasted. I always believe that everything happens at the perfect time.

~~~~~~~

Define yourself... I think we need to come up with our own definition of success and not let others define it for us. We can also fall into the trap of letting others set our goals for us. Some people define success as accumulating a vast amount of wealth or achieving wide recognition, but it's important to ask yourself, will these things make you truly happy? I believe success is when you feel content with who you are and what you offer to the world. I like this quote by John R. Wooden:

> *Success is peace of mind which is a direct result*
> *of self-satisfaction in knowing you did your best to*
> *become the best you are capable of becoming.*

If you want to be a doctor or a writer, the choice should be yours. Remember, you're the one who has to live your life—nobody else.

I am passionate about health and wellness. I feel strongly about understanding the true nature of our bodies and the essence of what life is about. To me there is nothing more exciting than studying ways in which we can make the most of who we are and the body we have been given.

~~~~~~~

Passion takes you places... Passion is something that can motivate you into action. Procrastination is something that prevents you from living your passion and ultimately deprives you of achieving your dreams. Be careful not to get stuck in the trap of procrastination! Procrastination is when you intend to do something but somehow never get around to doing it. We all know that feeling! You keep putting something off or you keep making up excuses not to do it.

By procrastinating you are reaffirming the belief that you can't achieve your goals. The first thing you should do so you can understand the real problem behind your procrastination is to identify those self-limiting beliefs that are holding you back. It could be that you don't think you have the skills to complete a project or that you're scared of failure. The only way to eliminate these limiting thoughts is through action, even if it may seem daunting at first. No successful man or woman you admire got to where they are by doing nothing. Say to yourself, "There is nothing stopping me from achieving my dreams!" Once you embrace your innermost passion, it will stay with you for life.

I like to surround myself with people who love life as much as I do. For me, the most interesting people are driven by their passion. If you are trying to find out what you are passionate about, look closely at the life you already lead. You might think back to what you dreamed about doing when you were a child or what you enjoy doing most today . . . it could be reading or writing, horse riding, cooking, helping people in all sorts of ways, looking at the way a car works—it could be anything! Your past might not point to the end of your quest, but it might take you to the next step.

Take some time to work out what really excites and inspires you. Discover what you would be prepared to do every day even for free! When you are following your passion, it won't even seem like work to you. Passionate people feel alive with their unwavering sense of direction in life. They exude an innate confidence and feel like they have total command of their world.

~~~~~~~

Getting Personal:
— What do you find easy to do?
— What comes naturally to you?
— What makes you smile?
— What do you like to talk about?
— What do you love about yourself?
— What are you confident about?
— What would you regret not doing?

rebecca

susie

lisa

brandi

mirror, mirror
on the wall

mum

Our physical appearance is a major part of our sense of self. Yet the definition of beauty is constantly changing. Not that long ago in the Western world, beauty was voluptuous, rounded hips and cherubic features. Tall women were considered too masculine and thin women too boyish. In some countries you are only pretty if you have fair skin and in others people spend all day in the sun trying to turn their skin golden brown. Beauty can never simply be restricted to one particular physical type, although it sometimes seems as though it is. Beauty is not something tangible that we can grasp and hold on to, it can be one of a million tiny things that push us into the "beauty box."

Beauty is within… Some people believe that who they are is just a reflection of what they see in the mirror. In order to be happy they need to be a foot shorter, have wider hips, a smaller nose, or a bigger bust size. They will wait forever to be happy. I've seen all different types of women with different body sizes, skin colors, and features, and I can honestly say that the women who stood out the most, who were really beautiful, were the ones who glowed from the inside.

Women who radiate inner beauty are attractive to everyone around them. Have you ever met a person who had "that something" that you couldn't quite put your finger on, but to whom you were just irresistibly drawn? It could be a man or a woman; one of your friends whom people just love to be around. Someone who can light up a room may not always be the most conventionally or fashionably "beautiful" person. They are, rather, someone who embraces what they've been given, and they accept and appreciate every part of themselves. Beauty is not only physical, it's a way of thinking about yourself—it comes from within.

~~~~~~~

The decision to be beautiful… I believe that being beautiful is a decision we make, a state of mind, and a way of being as opposed to a particular look or style. It's about knowing that you are worth loving. When a woman decides to be beautiful she radiates confidence and makes the most of her own traits and characteristics. I know so many women who might not fit the stereotypical, "conventional" idea of beauty, but you can see that they have simply decided to be beautiful regardless. As a result, they are doing what they want to do. These women are saying, "I embrace who I am and I'm proud of who I am."

There is no doubt that being happy about how we look is important. This means accepting the way we appear and making the most of it, even if it doesn't fit the world's standard of beauty. It's about looking within yourself and being honest. Embracing who you are means you will take better care of yourself and show the best of yourself to the world.

Is it easier for me to talk about being beautiful? It is not easier nor is it harder. I am a young woman who works as a model. I have been given what I have and I am doing the best with what I have been given. If I chose to, I could also spend my time wishing I looked different and comparing myself to other women around the world, but I realize that this is a waste of my time and energy. I am who I am, nothing more and nothing less, and so are you. It's about appreciating who you are as a unique individual. Ultimately you can choose to be beautiful and confident.

~~~~~~~

The model experience... What an experience modeling has been. There have been some great times and some sad and lonely times. It is interesting to me how modeling is perceived by many people. My own idea of what modeling was like was very different from the reality. I remember when I first started modeling, I thought that models got to choose what they wanted to wear in a shoot, lived a glamorous life, made lots of money, and were physically perfect. My opinion of myself was far from that. It's interesting looking back and realizing how much I have grown and changed as a person through my experiences in this industry. I want to share with you a few of the stories from my many years of modeling.

One of the very first trips I had for modeling was to Japan. I arrived to a model house full of European girls who didn't speak English, and I shared a room with one of them. The house wasn't that great. Things were really tough and everyone found it hard to make money. I remember eating rice a lot of the time. No one really bought much food because it would always go missing out of the fridge in the middle of the night, and no one would ever own up to taking it. Nor did they own up to taking clothes that didn't belong to them!

I was 17, nearly 18, and I was not so sure modeling was what I really wanted to do. I was in Japan for approximately two months. I celebrated my 18th birthday there. Being the first time I had been away from home on my birth-day, I missed my family, but the girls and the agency made my birthday special by throwing a surprise party for me. Despite this, after Japan I returned to Australia feeling like modeling wasn't for me.

I was doing the occasional modeling job but wasn't that interested in pursuing it any further, and I had been back in Australia for about a year, when the opportunity came up to go to Paris.

I lived in Paris for about six months. During one of the photo shoots there, toward the end of the shoot, my eyes starting hurting. The photographer had taken the protective layer off the flash and had it super close to my face. He told me to stare into it because we were shooting a beauty story and he wanted my eyes to sparkle. I mentioned to the photographer that this could not be good for my eyes and he told me it was fine. That night I ended up in the hospital vomiting from the pain. My eyes had been burned inside and had blistered. The doctor told me that I was lucky that I stopped work when I did. He likened my eyes being exposed to the continued bright flash to the burn from a welding flash that tradesmen sometimes get; the difference being that I had to endure continual flashes for most of the eight-hour shoot.

I left the hospital with patches on and ointment in my eyes. Thankfully, my boyfriend at the time was with me in Paris and I was lucky to have him there as he took care of me. I had to leave the patches on my eyes for ten days and could only remove them briefly to squeeze the burn ointment into them. Since I was a little girl I have always been afraid of the dark, and now I couldn't see and my world was in total darkness. I was unsure if my eyes were going to be okay and I was scared. I was on the other side of the world and so far away from my family. I thought about the situation then literally chose to create peace within myself. That's when I knew all would be okay. This experience made me appreciate my sight, something that I am so blessed to have.

The same experience happened to me again in New York, but thankfully it wasn't as bad! From these experiences I have learned to speak up when things don't seem to be right and to say an outright "No!" if there is something happening that I am not 100 percent happy about.

For ten years I flew around the world (I don't know how many times), the majority of the time flying economy class and going straight to work after 26 hours of travel, feeling extremely jet-lagged and tired. I've sat next to people who have fallen asleep and dribbled on my shoulder and almost snored the plane down. I've been vomited on by babies and sat next to children who have screamed the whole trip. I've sat next to people who want to talk your legs off when you are really tired and also people who just don't want to talk at all. It's been interesting to say the least and a lot of fun sometimes, but also exhausting.

In the last few years since I've been working with Victoria's Secret, I get to travel business or first class, and I can't tell you how fortunate I feel. I realize that a lot of people never get a chance to fly, let alone fly first class! I am grateful for the opportunities and experiences I have had.

A lot of girls out there strive to look like models. I think there is no such thing as looking like a model. Most of you would be surprised by how many different shapes, sizes, and looks you find with women in the modeling industry. And there's a big difference between the models you see in the magazines and what we actually look like in real life. Models don't wake up looking like they stepped off a magazine spread, or appear as fresh after a long, tiring day.

We go through hours of getting hair and makeup done as well as picking the most flattering outfit for our body type. Some people may be closer to the current idea of beauty but we still have freckles in odd places, dimples where we might not want them, and body parts we would like to change. There is no such thing as being picture perfect. Ultimately we are our harshest critics. Often we see our imperfections as limiting when others don't even notice them. If you can give up trying to "look good" or trying to "avoid looking bad" and just be authentically who you really are, a new level of freedom and self-expression will emerge. You get to be "real" not only with others, but most important, with yourself.

Try your best not to judge others. Judging people or feeling as though they are judging you are challenges worth overcoming. Sometimes people find it hard to believe that there's more to me than what they see on the outside. Part of my challenge to remain true to myself has been learning not to overcompensate for the preconceptions others might have about me.

It is easy to fall into the trap of judging someone based on your own ideas about what you feel others "should" be like, but in that process you fail to see who a person really is. Instead of judging people, I try to take time out to get to know and to speak with them. If people take the time to look beyond the outside they quite often find a different kind of person on the inside.

~~~~~~~

Fashion vs. style... For me, fashion and style are two separate things. Style is how you express your unique individuality; it's about the relationship you have with yourself. Fashion, on the other hand, is all about the clothes and their relationship to the world or the moment. So while I'm surrounded by fashion in my day-to-day life, I also have my own sense of style. Fashion is great, but I believe style forms part of your identity; the inner you expressed to the outer world.

Being beautiful on the outside doesn't mean that you automatically love who you are. Have you ever met people who seem to have it all but are never truly happy? You could be extremely attractive and still feel insecure and judged, and be a victim of self-criticism. Treasuring yourself is about changing limiting and negative thoughts. It's about being able to say, "I love and approve of myself."

It's not the way we look on the outside that matters, it's the way we feel on the inside that counts. It is important to accept ourselves for who we are; feel good about ourselves; and carry an inner strength so we can live a healthy, empowered, and productive life. Say to yourself, "When I embrace myself and treasure who I am, then love and respect flows into my life."

Knowing what you think about yourself is the first step toward challenging negative beliefs and thoughts. Replace negative beliefs with positive affirmations or power thoughts, which you can find in the second part of this book.

~~~~~~~

Getting Personal:

— How would you describe yourself physically to other people?

— How do you feel about your appearance?

— What do you like about the way you look?

— What is in your power to change easily?

Did you say more negative things about yourself or more positive things? Replace each negative thought with a positive one. Even if it feels a bit strange every time you think something negative, stop yourself and replace the negative with a positive statement.

One of my favorite poems for beauty advice is by Sam Levenson. It was one of Audrey Hepburn's favorites:

Time-Tested Beauty Tips

For attractive lips, speak words of kindness.

For lovely eyes, seek out the good in people.

For a slim figure, share your food with the hungry.

For beautiful hair, let a child run his
or her fingers through it once a day.

For poise, walk with the knowledge you'll never walk alone.

People, even more than things, have to be restored, renewed,

revived, reclaimed, and redeemed: never throw out anyone.

Remember, if you ever need a helping hand, you'll find one
at the end of your arm.

As you grow older you will discover that you have two

hands; one for helping yourself, the other for helping others.

The beauty of a woman is not in the clothes she wears,

the figure that she carries, or the way she combs her hair.

The beauty of a woman must be seen from in her eyes,

because that is the doorway to her heart, the place
where love resides.

The beauty of a woman is not in a facial mole,

but true beauty in a woman is reflected in her soul.

It is the caring that she lovingly gives,
the passion that she knows.

And the beauty of a woman, with passing years, only grows!

janine *judy* *margaret* *nan sanderson*

nan kerr

you are what you eat . . . and more!

Goodness comes from within—physical, mental, and spiritual. I feel you can't shine on the outside unless you are healthy on the inside. It's hard for your eyes to sparkle, your hair to shine, or your skin to glow if you are not truly healthy in mind, body and spirit. It's not just about food; it's about everything you put in and take out. It's giving and receiving equally.

As a model I have an extremely demanding schedule. I can be in up to six countries in the space of a ten-day period. The jetlag alone takes an enormous toll on my body. I know if I don't look after myself physically, emotionally, and spiritually then I won't be able to succeed in my career.

~~~~~~~

My healthy life... In the beginning, when I didn't have the nutritional knowledge I have now, I deprived myself of my favorite treats: chocolate, fried chicken, and ice cream. This just made me want them even more. Eventually I'd give in and eat twice as much, then feel bad about myself. Deciding that a certain food is "forbidden" will make you crave it more! My weakness is fried chicken. Although I know it's not good for me, and not just because of the calories, every now and again I'll treat myself. Moderation and knowing what's good for you are the keys to staying healthy and looking your best without feeling like you're deprived.

I've learned if I treasure myself and appreciate my body, I naturally want to fill it with all the right fuel so it can perform at its optimum. Educating myself about nutrition has made a huge difference as I can apply my knowledge daily. I eat the right food for my body, drink lots of water, and detox regularly. Now I rarely crave food that is not good for me, and when I do I allow myself a small portion and really enjoy it.

I have also found healthy alternatives that are highly
nutritious and sometimes even more satisfying.

~~~~~~~~

Fill your body with nutrients... and more. I
have been drinking a type of juice called Tahitian
noni juice daily since I was 13 years old—I love it.
It contains a large number of vitamins, minerals, and
antioxidants that I believe boost the immune system
and leave my skin feeling beautiful and soft. I've also
used this juice topically on my skin for years when
I've accidentally been sunburned or had pimples, and
it really helped. I recently created my own organic
skin-care line called Kora that contains noni juice.

Daily meditation ensures that I am healthy, alert,
and able to keep up with the demands of my job. I've
found that this, along with proper nutrition and exercise, makes me less susceptible to illness, and when
I do get sick I recover quickly, having given my body
the tools it needs to fight off illness or infection.

If you are having trouble keeping to your exercise program, try exercising with your friends. It's
easier as you tend to motivate each other into action, and it's also healthier than going for a cup of
coffee! What I practice keeps me fit and healthy in-

side and out, boosts my immune system, slows down the aging process, and allows me to be at my best at all times without the hassle of dieting. I use this affirmation: "I choose to fill my body with nutritious food and treasure my soul."

Yoga keeps me fit and healthy inside and out. It boosts the immune system, lubricates joints, massages the organs, and increases strength and flexibility as well as spiritual awareness. I believe it also slows down the aging process! My dear friend and yoga teacher Charlotte Dodson has taught me to honor my practice with quiet moments of positive intention, dedication, and gratitude. Through my daily yoga practice I've learned to concentrate on my breath. This helps me to truly be in the present moment, which is a gift to cherish. If my mind drifts away with thoughts, I intentionally bring my concentration back to my breath. After all, breath is the essence of life.

~~~~~~~

My top tips for staying healthy:
 — Focus on filling your body with nutrients instead of counting calories.
 — Fresh food is the best, so try to avoid processed food and artificial sweeteners, colors, and additives.

— Supplement your diet with a nutritional product that works for you.
— Try as much as possible to use natural and/or organic skin-care products and remedies.
— Establish a daily routine. For me that's body brushing, 20 minutes of power yoga, affirmations, and having a shower to my favorite song of the day.
— Sing, dance, smile and laugh. Nothing makes you feel so blessed as a big belly laugh. It is a great medicine, and it rejuvenates the soul.

~~~~~~~

Getting Personal:
— What is your daily routine like?
— Is there time in your routine to think about what you eat and drink?
— How can you start learning more about what you put into your body?
— What do you put on your body now?
— What can you do to better look after your health and yourself in general?

paddy   jaymee   judith   michelle

it's all about you

Balance is one of the key elements for your well-being. Try to imagine an old-fashioned weight scale: to balance the scales you need to put equal parts of your life on either side. Too much on one side will topple the scale, but when you place just the right amounts on either side, you find a force that's balanced and powerful.

When I lived in the model house I was way out of balance; sure, it was great to meet lots of girls from different parts of the world and have a sense of connection as we faced similar challenges, but it was really chaotic. So many people came and went; no one really nurtured the space we shared, and it felt really unsettling. I needed the complete opposite of what was going on.

Everyone needs a little time to nourish their soul and get back in touch with who they are and what they want. Sometimes the routine you have and the constant commitments you make throw you off the track of where you want to go. When I find myself in this place I try to make a concerted effort to make the time to do the things that I want to do. If you are constantly on the go, which I am, you can not only lose touch with the moment, you also run the risk of forgetting why you are doing what you do in the first place!

Ultimately, the more I think about it, living is not about doing but is more about *being*. For example, when a less-than-ideal situation arises, instead of getting angry or upset, I ask myself *"Who am I going to be in this situation?"* In that moment I create the possibility of, for example, "being" peaceful, calm, and loving no matter what; and as a result, I then get to choose how I react in any given situation. On the contrary, when I am "doing" and I react from that standpoint, I am at the effect of the situation and at the effect of everything happening around me. By choosing how I am going to "be" no matter what life throws at me, I get to live the life I choose.

It is also important to take time out to relax, appreciate, and reflect.

When you are in a relaxed state of mind you are able to see things more clearly, find a solution to that problem you were mulling over, and even just reaffirm where you are and where you want to be. When you are calm, relaxed, and peaceful, you get back in touch with who you are.

When I need to relax, music can completely change the way I feel and the mood I'm in. I dance and sing around the house or in my hotel room. I love losing myself in music and giving myself the opportunity to completely switch off and think about nothing else. It is like a moving meditation. Another thing I enjoy is being with nature. Whenever I can, I spend time barefoot in the grass or just resting against a tree. These small moments help me balance and reconnect with the greater energies in nature, giving me a sense of my place in the world.

~~~~~~~

My tips for getting balance in your life:
— Pamper yourself and get a massage or take a bath.
— Spend time with your pets.
— Spend time in nature: at parks, beaches, or just in the garden. Take your shoes off and connect with Mother Nature.
— Make sure you get enough sleep during the night. Otherwise take a short power nap during the day.

— Meditate or sit quietly, just focusing on your breath for 20 minutes.
— Get some exercise! Exercise is a great way to release endorphins, feel-good chemicals in the body that reduces stress.
— Be productive. Make a list of the things you have to do for the day and organize the list by importance. In this way you can take care of things before they become a problem.

~~~~~~~

Living in the moment... When you are feeling balanced you'll find that you are also centered on the present moment. This is something I believe is invaluable if you want to be more relaxed and in control of your life. When some people think about being in the present moment, they might jump to the conclusion that you have to be passive and forget your goals, the past, and the future—but this is not the case. Living in the moment is letting go of all that stress and worry that you have accumulated and not projecting those negative emotions on your future actions. It's more about working actively towards your goals and dreams without constantly stressing about how you are going to achieve them or replaying past mistakes in your head. In this way, we don't judge the moment we are in but accept it for what it is.

This is something that really works for me. It would be very easy for me to remember all the times I have made mistakes in the past and let it affect the job I am doing in the present, especially when it comes to modeling, because if you are constantly worried and stressed on a job it shows! Making an effort to be completely in the present helps me to focus my attention on the task ahead without letting my negative emotions influence the way I behave.

Every moment that we enter is like a blank canvas; it's our emotions and thoughts that color what we see. When you are in the present moment it's easier to accept the reality of the situation that you are in. When you embrace the way things are in the moment, you start the process of change, and you allow new possibilities to emerge.

~~~~~~~

Getting Personal:
— Is your life in balance?
— What do you need to let go of to become more balanced?
— How can you create more balance?

alison

hayley

margaret

the green-eyed monster

carlotta

Jealousy can be a powerful emotion if it is given the opportunity to spiral out of control. You won't be able to slay this monster with a traditional sword and shield, and you definitely can't close your eyes and hope it goes away. At some point everyone has experienced jealousy and envy, and it doesn't feel good.

My transient and hectic lifestyle can often cause me to feel insecure and unsure of myself. If I don't find ways of grounding myself, it's easy to get caught up in hurtful games. I choose not to get involved if I feel someone is encouraging such negative feelings. Of course, it's not always easy, and I try to be mindful about my responses.

Like everybody, I too have had my bouts of jealousy throughout my life. Once, when my boyfriend at the time told me
he preferred blondes, I really took that to heart. Every time
I saw him talking to a blonde, I got jealous and upset. This
concerned me as I didn't want to be jealous, so I took a look
within. I saw that I wasn't being powerful in how I was react-
ing. I realized that if he wanted to be with a blonde he would
be with a blonde, but he chose me. I decided to trust and
appreciate our relationship and my own uniqueness.

Practicing yoga and meditation, which help create balance
internally, gives me a sense of happiness within myself. Now if
I ever feel a twinge of jealousy, I take a deep breath and really
be with those feelings. Once you accept those feelings and sit
with them, I find they generally pass. If that doesn't work, I put
my thoughts and feelings on paper as openly and honestly as I
can. This gives me the opportunity to see my thoughts in black
and white, release whatever I was thinking about, and bring
myself back into balance.

I believe jealousy is all about negative power and attention.
The core of jealousy is inadequacy. Jealousy is present when
our sense of self is put at risk. When we feel this emotion it
is akin to having an identity crisis, and it is a calling within us
to better ourselves. I believe that all our emotions are there to
show us who we are and jealousy is no exception. If you are
truly comfortable in your own skin and confident in your own
abilities, you can transform jealousy into acceptance.

Jealousy is not the same as healthy competition. When it comes to success in sports or business, healthy competition can motivate and push you to achieve your goals. But when it comes to being competitive about looking better, dressing better, or sounding better than someone else, I'd take a step back. I think those sorts of games bring out the worst in yourself and other people, and only encourage the games to keep going on. I use this affirmation to help me avoid getting caught up: "I allow people to be what they want to be. I accept and love others unconditionally."

It is important to remind ourselves that we are all perfect exactly the way we are. We all have strengths and weaknesses, and we also have all the resources we need to improve ourselves. We have the responsibility to ourselves to discover what makes us distinctive and to further develop our talents. It doesn't help to wait for the approval of others to feel good. Work on accepting yourself as you are, and become the best version of you that you can be.

We are all unique flowers in this garden of life. We need to embrace our uniqueness and not compare ourselves with others. A rose is as beautiful in its own way as a daisy and a sunflower. They are unique. It's not until we fully understand, embrace, and accept our individuality that we will truly shine.

~~~~~~

My tips for dealing with jealousy:
— Identify what is making you jealous and why.
— Sit with it and accept it.
— Instead of focusing on the negative feeling jealousy can produce, look at it as an act of motivation. By doing this you will be less likely to concentrate on the things you don't have, and develop the drive to obtain the things you want.
— Take time to appreciate what you have.
— Get it out of your system. Write down how you feel or talk to someone about it. This is better than letting these feelings bottle up where they can do more damage.
— Stop comparing yourself with others. Always keep in mind that everybody is different and unique in their own way. Make a conscious effort to think about your own good qualities and your own uniqueness.
— Be accepting of yourself.

~~~~~~~

Getting Personal:

— Who are you jealous of?

— What is underneath your feelings of jealousy?

— How can you transform these negative feelings into positive action for yourself?

carlii

sonia

lauren

sally

relationships are your strengths

romy

Relationships in your life can vary from smooth and easy to temperamental and challenging. They don't just begin and jump straight to "happily ever after." Relationships take time, acceptance, and effort to grow into something beautiful. I have found that the best relationships are founded on trust, honesty, and communication. If one of these elements is lacking, relationships crumble. I strongly believe that the beliefs and values you hold about yourself and your life are reflected in all your relationships. Your relationships with others can tell you a lot about yourself.

Sometimes when I'm facing challenges in a relationship, I wonder if I would be better off being on my own to find peace.

Then I realize it is precisely those challenging relationships that help me become a better version of myself.

Relationships force us to look at our least desirable qualities or traits so we can recognize them. Just as rocks bumping into each other in a stream eventually polish each other smooth, life polishes us through the challenges of our relationships.

This does not mean we should stay in relationships that we've outgrown. Sometimes the highest way to honor ourselves is to walk away when the relationship no longer meets our needs. One of the hardest things I've had to do in my career was change agents. This was a difficult decision to make, as my agent was someone I was personally fond of. In the end I needed to let the relationship go, though, because it wasn't satisfying my business needs.

~~~~~~~

Respect yourself... If you don't respect yourself, how can you expect others to? If you are continually beating yourself up about every mistake you've ever made, the people around you will focus on the same and criticize you as well. Once you begin to value yourself, others will start to value you, too. The truth is, if you treasure yourself, everyone else around you will recognize your worth. The people in your life will only treat you as well as you treat yourself. This applies to any type of relationship you have with other people, and is sometimes especially obvious with a romantic one.

My advice when it comes to dating is to be true to yourself and know what you want. If a date doesn't call you back, realize that it's obviously not meant to be and let it go. After a bad dating experience, be in control of the things you are thinking about, and you'll realize that your thoughts are creating your reality and the way you feel. You can either start picking apart the relationship and everything that went wrong, or you can learn from what happened and be a better person for it.

~~~~~~~

Mending a broken heart... In my experience, when a relationship ends, I try to take it day by day. Some days I'd rather be alone, while at other times I am in the mood to go out dancing or hang out with my friends. It's okay to get upset and go with your emotions instead of fighting them, while keeping in mind that you can get through this. It's like going through any other personal journey, there are always going to be ups and downs along the way. It's important to remember that you're a unique person with plenty of gifts to offer the world. Don't forget all the other relationships you have—with your friends and family.

Because I'm so busy there are times when I don't even get the chance to really sit and think about what is happening in my personal life. Sometimes this can be a blessing in disguise, for a while at least. However, ultimately you can never escape the healing process, no matter how busy you are. Breakups are never easy, but they have given me some of my best life lessons. Once I've had a chance to reflect, I could see how I have grown as a person and how it has inevitably made me stronger.

I believe that every relationship comes into your life for a reason, and it is important not to compare them because they are always going to be different. It is a journey that you travel together where you enjoy the experiences and love that you share. Relationships can really teach you a lot about yourself. It's important to reflect and focus on yourself and what you want before you get involved with someone else. Taking some time out and getting to know yourself is vital to ensuring you make better choices next time. You are the person you are today because of the experiences that have occurred in your life. Take a moment to think about all your past relationships and the valuable lessons they have taught you. If anything, you should have a clearer knowledge of what you *don't* want.

Don't look for someone else to complete you; likewise, don't look for partners who think they need someone to complete them. We are all whole and complete just as we are. Looking for happiness through someone else ultimately leads to disappointment, as only *you* can make *you* happy.

~~~~~~~

Flying solo... Being fulfilled as a person doesn't always mean you have to be in a romantic relationship. In fact, it can be great to be single! Try to live in the moment and engage with every aspect of your life. Take the time to do the things you want to and like to do. For me that means dancing, yoga, hiking, enjoying good food with great company, or writing. Ask yourself what are the things you most enjoy doing? Pursue your passions whatever they may be, because whether you're single or with a partner, your life's goals and dreams are your own and will energize you and make life more meaningful. Sometimes when you are in a relationship, it can be easy to forget the things that you want to do as an individual. You can be so focused on being a couple that when you are no longer in a relationship it's harder to find your feet again. This is a good opportunity for reconnecting and getting back in touch with yourself and what you need. You also have the time to maintain contact with the friendships that are important to you. It's good to always remember that you are not alone. There are other people around you who are also enjoying the journey of flying solo.

~~~~~~

The power of friendship... My friendships are a strength that I know I can rely on. When I have true, meaningful friendships in my life, I know I have the support to handle anything that comes my way. I've always thought that friends are the angels that are sent down to help you along your life's path. They bring encouragement, understanding, strength, fun, and laughter. Besides, my family I know exactly who I'd call if there was something I wanted to share or if I needed advice. Romantic relationships may come and go, but true friends will always be there for you.

I've learned that the friendships that do stick are the ones that are about giving as well as receiving. If you want a great friend, you also have to be a great friend! Look yourself in the eye—would you be friends with you? Being a great friend means being a great listener, being trustworthy, and knowing when to give advice and when to just be there. I don't always agree with my friends' opinions and views when it comes to certain things, and they don't always agree with mine. And that's okay, as it makes each person in the relationship interesting. We all have arguments with those who are close to us, and it's important to remember not to get caught up in petty disagreements. Don't create "stories" about what happened; rather, rely on fact and be authentic and honest when dealing with any disagreement and actually see it for what it is. Sadly, most people's stories about what happened become their reality, and as a result things get blown out of all proportion. See a disagreement for what it is and don't add meaning to it. If a relationship is something that you value, then it is worth mending.

~~~~~~~

Learning to let go... I have found that throughout my life, as I have changed and grown from each new experience, some of my friends around me have also changed. At first this used to bother me, as the people I used to be close with were no longer in my life. What I eventually realized was that as my values and beliefs evolved, I began to attract like-minded people. Some of my friends are on a journey similar to mine, and I know they are the friends I will have for a lifetime. Others are markers on the road that point me in the right direction or travel with me for a while until I or they choose another path. I appreciate and value both kinds, as all the people in my life have added to the person I am today. I was once told that if you wanted to see what type of person someone is, you just have to look at their friends. It's important to be around people who mirror the real you and not to change who you are to fit in with other people. In the end real friends accept you for who you are and walk in when others walk out.

~~~~~~~

Getting Personal:
— What do your relationships tell you about yourself?
— How could they be different?
— What changes can you make to have better
  relationships?

69

charlotte   lilly   marija   ashlee

it's like magic

liesel

I believe that the stronger the energy or attention you give something, the more it magnifies in your life. Think of this in terms of light. If your focus is soft like torchlight, your achievements may be small and unclear. If your focus is like a laser beam, then some interesting things start to happen. The greatest achievers in this world focus their attention in this way and accomplish some amazing things. How you focus *your* attention will determine *your* experience.

You may think you're not destined for amazing things, but life could bring you unexpected opportunities. Think about the things that you want to have in your life: a new job, traveling to a new country, or finding your soul mate. Whenever I have a goal that I want to achieve, I first determine how much I really want it. If my desire for it is a five on a scale out of ten, then I know I'm not really going to put enough energy into getting it. But if I want it a lot, it becomes a priority or a goal that I work toward.

~~~~~~~~

Use what you have... For a long time I felt ambiguous about modeling. I had a lot of preconceived ideas about what it was like, and to be honest I felt embarrassed about being a model. After all, I wasn't finding a cure for cancer, saving the rainforests, or working for world peace! Then my dad reminded me that I have the opportunity to use what I do right now and all that I have learned, and transform that into doing something I really think is worthwhile. I can use my profile as an international model to draw attention to what I think is important in life and share my experiences and journey. This helped me really embrace what I do right now and appreciate the marvelous opportunities I have.

Two charities I am currently supporting are The Koala Foundation and Kids Helpline, and I know there will be others that I will also support.

Once you've begun to change the way you think and draw the things you want into your life, you can think about how what you do can benefit others around you.

The important thing to remember is that what you do doesn't have to be some grand gesture. Something as simple as offering love and nurturing the health and well-being of another living creature can have amazing results. When I first got my dog, Frankie, she was a tiny, shy, shivery little thing. I poured all my love and attention on her and within weeks she transformed into a joyful, happy, healthy puppy, and now brings happiness and love to everyone she meets. It's not necessary to wait for some big project; every small thing you do can have the power to transform your life. Once you start something positive, it will ripple outward and has the potential to touch the lives of others.

My mum always said to me, "If you are going to do something, do it properly." It's not too profound, really quite simple, yet this thought has been very powerful for me. It has influenced the way I approach every area of my life. If I am going to invest my time and energy into something, then I make sure I give it my all. I know that at the end of the day I couldn't have done a better job and that I have the full experience of doing something the right way. Gaining confidence and welcoming challenges means you'll be more aware of what you want to do. Doing things halfheartedly because someone else thinks you should means you're robbing yourself of achieving your desires and dreams. If you give something your full attention, you will always receive the greatest benefit.

~~~~~~~

My tips for making magic:

1. **Create, and when creating remember**: *The context is decisive*. What I mean by this is that ultimately, whatever you create for yourself or whatever space you choose to be in, you will reap what you sow. Like attracts like. If you

choose to be positive, positive things will happen. If you choose to live in the negative, you will attract negative things. So instead focus and create good, and good things will happen in your life.

2. Focus your intention. Choose the most important thing you want to achieve at this moment. Write it down clearly and succinctly as though you've already achieved it. For example, "I am healthy" has more power than saying "I wish to be healthy." "I am surrounded by supporting and loving friends" has greater power than "I want to be supported and loved by my friends." "I am living in a wonderful apartment not too far from work and that I can easily afford" has greater power than "I want to live in an apartment not too far from work and that I can easily afford." The words you use are central to achieving your intention.

3. Create a vision board. Be creative with your goal. Get a large white piece of cardboard, and write your goal at the top. Draw, write, or stick pictures from magazines or anything else to the board that represents your goal. I love color so I use magazine cuttings, colored pens, and paint. Place your vision board where you can see it all the time. My favorite place is in my bedroom, where I can look at it and imagine all those things in my life before I go to sleep.

4. Take action now! Remember to focus all your energy on your intention. You won't top the class if you don't apply yourself. You aren't going to meet the love of your life on your couch! Nor will you land that great job without some training and effort. Do some research on how you can achieve your goal. Take a course or ask your family or friends to help. Whenever you have doubts, look at your vision board to remind yourself why you want to achieve this in your life. Think about yourself having it and how this would make you feel. Really bring those feelings to life within you: happiness, satisfaction, achievement, joy. Close your eyes and imagine reaching your goal. This should give you the motivation you need to get back on track.

Most important, know that you are worthy and that you have everything you need inside you, all the tools you'll ever require, to have the life that you want. All you need is a healthy dose of determination, a significant measure of focus, a sprinkle of passion, and a couple of handfuls of positivity!

~~~~~~~

Getting Personal:
— Is your energy focused or scattered?
— What is your most important goal right now?
— What do you need to do to keep your energy focused on achieving this goal?

danielle

sianna

maz

brooke

don't forget to
say "thank you"

nan smith

Gratitude unlocks the fullness of life. It turns what we have into enough, and more. It turns denial into acceptance, chaos to order, confusion into clarity. It can turn a meal into a feast, a house into a home, a stranger into a friend. Gratitude makes sense of our past, brings peace for today, and creates a vision for tomorrow.

— Melody Beattie

Gratitude is everything... Being grateful helps create a positive attitude. Gratitude shifts your focus from what you don't have to all that you do have. I try my best to live from the point of gratitude, which means focusing on the positives, and share my life and its rewards when I can.

Whenever I am tired or maybe feeling a little sorry for myself I make a mental note of all the things I have to be grateful for. Gratitude helps me when I'm on a swimwear shoot and it's snowing, or when I'm getting up at 4 a.m. for work. I remind myself that everything I do is moving me toward my goals. Being grateful gives me an immediate boost in energy and brings me back into the moment.

There are many things in my life that fill me with gratitude. All the love in my life, my family, and my friends, old and new, are at the top of my list. Being Australian and growing up in such a naturally beautiful country is something I deeply appreciate. Having the opportunity to travel the world and visit amazing places while experiencing different cultures and meeting interesting people is something I truly treasure. I have a healthy body, eyes to see the world, and a voice to speak my mind. I am grateful for my career, all the people I have met along the way, and a wonderful support team. I am also grateful for my gorgeous little dog, Frankie, who is such a ray of sunshine in my life.

Simply being grateful can change your whole perspective on life. If ever I am having a bad day or if things aren't going quite to plan and I feel like giving up on my dreams, I take a step outside my world and then I get to see just how lucky I am. I encourage you to do that. Next time you are feeling down, take a trip to a mall, a homeless shelter, or a children's hospital and take a look around. When we take time to acknowledge everything around us, we get to appreciate just how lucky we really are. Being grateful allows me to see life for what it is and gives me the opportunity to live in every moment. You'll find that once you make a conscious effort to be grateful, you're happier and the things that might have been depressing or stressful before don't factor in as often. Being grateful is actually good for your health. When I remind myself of everything I am grateful for I no longer have the need to dwell on the past or worry about the future. I realize that all that has happened is finished and all that will happen is ultimately part of my path moving forward. The moment I am feeling ungrateful I take a walk outside for a reality check.

Gratitude can come from the smallest experience. Once, during an exhausting day, I was feeling annoyed about some extra work I had to do, so I stepped inside my dressing room to take a break and collect my thoughts. Playing on the television screen was a movie I had just seen the week before, *The Pursuit of Happyness* starring Will Smith. This particular scene had Will Smith's character and his son spending the night on the floor of a public bathroom because he didn't have any other place to go and was struggling to find work to take care of his son. Being reminded of that one scene changed my attitude immediately and reminded me to appreciate everything in my life and not to take anything for granted.

~~~~~~~

Dealing with negativity... Handling negativity within yourself, with others, or in particular situations is challenging. I do my best to rise above it and focus on the people in my life who are supportive. It is the negative people in the world who give you the opportunity to be really grateful for all the nurturing and wonderful people that surround you. The things that matter to me the most are people and nature; nothing is more important to me than showing my love and appreciation for the people in my life and the natural environment that surrounds and nourishes me.

A great way to focus on being more grateful is to keep a gratitude journal, which you can write in every day. In this way not only are we more aware of the good things in our life by writing them down, but we also remember the contribution of others and how we fit into the bigger picture. One day you can write about how grateful you are for your apartment that you live in and all the things you enjoy about having your own place. Another entry might be about how much you appreciate your friends and family. You can even write about the delicious breakfast you had that morning! I'm especially grateful for the times during the day that I can step outside and feel the sun on my skin and take a moment to breathe in the fresh air. When I remind myself of this moment, it triggers the memory and I almost feel like I'm there again. The best way to go about this is if you try to be creative and think outside the box. You might have five main things you are grateful for every day, but make it a point to try to notice the unexpected things that you can appreciate and be grateful for.

Sometimes it's even helpful if you take a minute to look at the difficult times you've been through. When I think of something challenging that has happened, whether it is something personal or professional, I can look at where I am now and see how far I have come and how much I have grown from every experience along the way.

~~~~~~~

Getting Personal:
— What are you grateful for?
— What are the positive things in your life right now?
— What or who inspires you?
— How can you show your gratitude more often?

alison

lauren

leanne

the glass is always half full

venya

The benefit of being positive is something that we hear continuously. Best-selling authors have written about it, psychologists have published papers on this topic, and no doubt you've heard it pop up from time to time in conversation. "Be positive," "stay positive," and "you need to have a positive attitude," have become standard phrases that we use when appropriate . . . but what does it actually mean?

What gave me a clearer outlook on this was some research that Dr. Masaru Emoto conducted on water crystals. Dr. Emoto did a study on how energy, thoughts, words, and even music affected water. He started by freezing a tiny portion of water that had been taken from various parts of the world and photographing their molecular structures. He made some amazing discoveries on how saying or even thinking words of love and gratitude around water could change water's structure into something like the form of a beautiful snowflake, and how saying negative words could make the water structure look eroded and splotchy. Taping words such as *hope, peace, thank you,* and *I love you* to glasses of water had a profound effect almost immediately, as well as words like *hate, you fool,* and *sick.*

Scientists have long proven that everything is made out of energy. If we break things down we can see how matter is made out of atoms, and if you break that down further you'd see that atoms are just vibrating energy. It's the same with water and also with our bodies. This study on water made such an impact on me because it is a fact that approximately 70 percent of the average person is made up of water! Our thoughts and words can have a profound effect on our bodies, too.

~~~~~~~~

Affirmations… Feeding my mind with positive thoughts is just as important to me as feeding my body with fresh organic food and nutrients. I have my affirmations by the bedside so that as soon as I wake up I can randomly select some to read. Sometimes just one will help me set the mood for the entire day. I decide to really "be" the affirmation and live that thought for the day. By making affirmations a part of my everyday life, I feel more centered and inspired.

If ever I am feeling off balance, these positive statements remind me of the truth. I have them written down everywhere, whether in my diary or on little pieces of paper, and will read over them every chance I get. There is a list of affirmations on the back of my front door so that I can read them before leaving the house. I feel as though this prepares me mentally and emotionally for the day ahead. In my room, a beautiful wooden chest contains my written dreams and goals as well as pictures of places I would like to visit and treasures I would love to have in my life.

Having a positive attitude gives me the energy to keep up with my schedule and give the best of myself to whatever I have to do. Most important of all, a positive attitude allows me to be confident, feel uplifted, and make the most of every situation I am confronted with. Being positive gives me choices and power in my decisions, and direction in life. When I choose to look at things with a positive perspective, I tend to be more willing to act when something occurs as opposed to feeling helpless and out of control.

Louise Hay puts words together beautifully, and when I'm reading her books and affirmation cards, her love and warmth comes through. Her book *You Can Heal Your Life* made me realize just how powerful thoughts can be and that no matter how healthy your diet and lifestyle is, if there is negativity, you not only create disease in your mind and body, you also invite more negativity into your life. What you put out you get back. Whenever I catch myself in negative self-talk, or jumping to conclusions and assumptions about things, I remind myself that in the end I have the choice in the thoughts I want to listen to.

~~~~~~~

Don't worry… be happy! It is easy to get caught up in worrying about what's going on in your life and the thoughts and opinions of others. In my industry it's especially easy to get sucked into worrying about the way you look on a shoot, what you said in that interview, or even if that decision you made was the right one. I can find myself worrying so much about some of these things that I forget to really enjoy the moment and have fun. If I find that I simply can't turn my mind from stressing about a particular thing, I just tackle the problem head on and change my thinking. I find it helpful to ask myself the following questions:

1. *Are there any reasons for me to worry?* In this way I can determine if my view is realistic and balanced.

2. *Is there another reason for why I'm getting stressed?*

3. *What is the worst that could happen?* If you know that you can still survive after this, then everything else becomes easier to handle. I then think about the best possible scenario and then the most realistic one.

4. *How would I feel if I stopped worrying?* This helps to bring me back to the present and reminds me that I have the choice to feel better.

~~~~~~~~

Let your light shine... There was a time when I seriously considered giving up my career. I was feeling down, and it seemed as though nothing was going right. I had just returned from working in Paris, which had not been as successful as I hoped, and I began to doubt my abilities. Just when I was about to walk away from everything, the words my mum always said at the end of each phone conversation, "Let your little light shine," came to mind. It was then I realized I was the one turning off my light with so many low-energy thoughts.

Whenever I find myself feeling low, I think about shining a light. It reminds me that the most important thing in these times is to stay true to who you are. Trying to convince others you're beautiful, desirable, and confident won't work unless it comes from an inside knowingness. When you turn on your inner light and let it glow, it's like switching on a light in the darkness. You effortlessly begin to attract all sorts of interesting creatures.

Convince yourself, not others, that you're warm and bright. *Be* warm and bright and everyone will be attracted to you. You don't have to say a word to convince them; the attraction will be irresistible because of your positive, bright outlook about yourself and the world. That night in Paris I made a commitment to transform my thinking and keep my inner light shining. I truly believe it is why I have been able to achieve what I have today. In changing the way I was thinking, I transformed the way I felt and also what I thought of my abilities and myself. I therefore altered my reality and started making choices to surround myself with positivity in every shape and form. As I began to value myself more, I noticed a remarkable shift for the better in my life.

One of the most dramatic ways you can transform any given situation is to rethink your attitude. To this day, Mum still says, "Let your little light shine," and her saying that always make me feel better and empowers me to look at and appreciate all the positives in my life. Attitude really is everything.

~~~~~~~

Finding your power... The rest of this book contains power thoughts to motivate and encourage you to live an abundant and confident life. They are from some of the people who have been an inspiration to me, such as Louise Hay, Deepak Chopra, and Dr. Wayne W. Dyer, to name a few. Then I added my own affirmations to every power thought to make them more relevant for you. Whatever mood or situation you find yourself in, there will be at least one power thought that can help you move toward a more positive frame of mind. You can use this book in many ways—here are some of my suggestions for how to make the most of them:

1. Find the power thought to bring about change and give you the positive feeling you desire.

2. Hold the book in your hands and then let your intuition guide you to open up to the page you are meant to read. This will be the power thought that will bring positive energy to your situation.

3. Flip through the book and find the power thought that you want to use for the moment. For example, if you want to feel more confident right now, then "I release all fears and doubts" would work for you.

4. Use a power thought to change your life while sleeping. Simply read the power thought a few times in your head before bedtime, and then repeat the thought over and over again until you fall asleep.

To really get the most out of these power thoughts, repetition is the key. Think of them as an internal exercise program to build your strength so you can face any challenge that comes your way. Louise Hay once told me that whenever someone has a limiting thought they can turn it around with an affirmation. These power thoughts are like planting a seed. If you were going to plant your heart, what would grow? The positive thought or desire may not necessarily be true right then, but it is something that you would like to be true. Finding the courage to plant the seed creates miracles. You may not see all the benefits on the first day, but as you use them consistently, the inner you will get into shape.

rose marie

jane

lilly

dream your
way to success

tahli

I love my sleep and my dreams, so one of my favorite ways to use power thoughts is while I'm asleep. Dreams can be used to solve problems—just think of the phrase "I'll sleep on it"! Each of us dreams in our own unique way. By using power thoughts, you can program your dreams so that when you wake up, you'll already be in a more positive frame of mind and able to greet the day with a smile.

Dreams are such an important part of my life, and over the years I have kept journals to write down my dreams and shared them with my friends and family. Decoding them can also be a lot of fun and very insightful. Dreams help us become more balanced, and when we wake up we often forget what we were dreaming and are just left with an emotion. My friend Leon Nacson, a renowned Dream Coach, developed the system, which I use often, to develop positive affirmations to program our dreams and at the same time have an effect on our waking life.

Here is how it works: If you're looking for a change and know exactly which power thought serves the purpose, then go straight to the relevant page. If you are looking for a general pick-me-up or you are not sure what will quench your uneasiness, choose a page at random. Write the power thought down, read it to yourself, and then place it under your pillow. As you are falling asleep, keep repeating this power thought as many times as you can. When you wake up, the very first thing you do is repeat the power thought. This is a very powerful way of reinforcing affirmations. I've chosen a few of the affirmations that I use regularly from Leon's card deck that have worked for me.

~~~~~~~

Make your own power thoughts... At the end of the book, there are some personal power thoughts that I have written myself. You can create your own, too, specifically to suit your needs. Here are some guidelines to create an effective power thought:

— Choose a phrase that describes what you desire. Short, powerful statements work much better than long, drawn-out paragraphs.

— Your statement must be in the present tense. For example, use "I am passionate about school/my career" instead of "I will be passionate about school/ my career." The first is working on changing your present circumstances, while the latter indicates some point in the future and that might leave you always waiting!

— Your power thought should always stem from a positive perspective instead of a negative one. For example, don't use "I don't like my career when I'm not passionate about it," as this places your career in a negative light. Always phrase your power thoughts in a positive way: "I am always passionate about my career" is much stronger.

— Your power thought should always be said in the first person, which is "I." This is because the power thought is always about you. You can't use a power thought about another person, because you can only affect your own reality. Happiness has to come from within you before it can extend to and from other people.

~~~~~~~

Keep moving... anything is possible. Keep this book close to you: on your bedside table, in your bag, on your desk. Choose a power thought or several every morning, and decide which one will keep you moving toward your goals and dreams today.

A lot of the thoughts and ideas in this book have come not only from my experiences but also from the wisdom of others. Being not even 30 years old, I still have a lot of life experiences ahead of me, and I'm sure I will come across a lot more challenges along the way. Life is a continuous journey, and there will always be more lessons to learn, more journeys to take, and more people who will impact my life in various ways. I know what I have learned so far and will learn in the future will help guide me throughout my life.

I hope that some of these thoughts resonate with you the way they resonated with me when they came across my path, and help you get through the challenges you may face along your way. Like the butterfly, always remember that there is something beautiful waiting on the other side, no matter how much resistance you encounter.

And always remember, when you Treasure Yourself, life will reflect that back to you.

My mum used to make my brother and me special cakes
for our birthdays. This was my third birthday.

was about ten and a half in this photo below, and I was going to my first ever school dance. I was so nervous. At this time I hadn't fully accepted myself for who I was. I felt self-conscious and quite shy.

One of my first ever photoshoots. This was for
DOLLY magazine. I was nearly 14. I still hadn't come into my
own yet, but was starting to break through my shell.

Nan and Pa have blessed my life in more ways than I could possibly imagine. They are amazing, beautiful people, and I love them both so much.

This is one of my favorite photos of Chris (my first boyfriend) and me. It was taken in 1998 at his family's home about five months before he die

Frankie and me in New York City not long after I moved there. Frankie is such a beautiful little soul.

One of my first ever fashion shoots for Victoria's Secret.
It was shot in Venezuela in Los Roques. It was the
first time I'd met some of the VS angels; they were
so beautiful, and I was still a little unsure of myself.

The other girls and me on our way from NYC to LA for the VS Show in 2006. This was my first ever fashion show for Victoria's Secr

(left) This is me onstage in Los Angeles for the Victoria's Secret Show. I was really nervous, yet really excited at the same time. Each step I had taken had brought me to this point, where I'd become more comfortable in my own skin.

This is me at a charity event in New York City. It was so rewarding to spend some time with these beautiful young people.

Louise Hay has been an inspiration to me for so long.
Here we are in Sydney, Australia, in 2008.

2008: This was my first
Harper's Bazaar Cover.
It was for Harper's UK
and was shot by
Michelangelo Di Battista.

My third Victoria's Secret Show, my first time wearing angel wings.
How crazy is it that they were actually butterfly wings?

This was shot for
V Magazine by
Willy Vanderperre.
It was a totally
different look
from what people
were used to
seeing me as.

Платье из атласа, платье
и шорты из хлопка, все
Prada; юбки из хлопка,
все архив студии Warner
Bros. LA; туфли из атласа,
Miu Miu; носки из хлопка,
Raf Simons Archive.

Shot in the South of France. This was for *Vogue*.

KORA™ Organics by Miranda Kerr

It was my vision to create my own organic skin-care line.
It stems from my passion and love of organics. I have created
the skin care that I personally love and use.

Prada Fashion Show
Milan, 2010
What an incredible
experience.

Balenciaga Fashion Show. Paris, 2010. This was my second
Balenciaga show; it was an honor to be part of it again.

This is a recent shot of my family and me. I don't know
where I would be without them.

Thank you for being the best mother ever,
my best friend, and for your unconditional love.

affirmations i love...

and how you can incorporate
them into the script of your life.

i am willing to change.

— louise l. hay

i flow freely with change and welcome
the opportunities it brings. as i grow and
experience new things, i create the space
for positive thoughts and actions to arise.

i stand strong in my personal power.

— deepak chopra

i am a creative human being with unlimited
potential. i create a space for anything i want
in my life to appear, and i appreciate and
seize every opportunity.

i am worth loving.

i honor and accept myself as the unique human
being i am. i am content, alive, and worthy.
i give and receive love unconditionally.

i know that my way is not the only way.

— brian l. weiss, m.d.

each day i am open to the endless
possibilities the universe has in store for me.
i listen, acknowledge, and choose powerfully
what opportunities i take, appreciating
all that is offered.

i am willing to forgive.

— louise l. hay

i put the past behind me, and i open my
life to the endless freedom available through
forgiveness. i give myself permission to forgive
and greet the possibilities now available to me
with an open, loving heart.

i uplift everyone i meet.

— miranda kerr

i choose to focus on people's
positive traits and encourage
them to do the same.

*i turn every experience
into an opportunity.*

— louise l. hay

experiences, good or bad, are opportunities
to learn and grow. i acknowledge that life's
experiences have and will continue to shape
and create the unique human being i am.

i think before i speak.

— brian l. weiss, m.d.

i acknowledge that words have the ability to
impact other people's lives. i think before
i speak, and i speak words of support,
compassion, and love to all.

i trust my inner wisdom.

— louise l. hay

my intuition guides me through my life.
my inner voice is wise and knows
what's best for me.

i cannot be a victim and be happy.

— robert holden

i am a powerful human being capable of
achieving my dreams. i am content and happy
with my life. nothing constrains me. i choose
each day to live my life and achieve my dreams.

*i deserve the best and
i accept the best now.*

— louise l. hay

i appreciate and value all that i have.
i am empowered, and i create daily the life
i choose and enjoy the best life has to offer me.
i have an amazing, fulfilling life, and
i deserve the best.

my life is supposed to be fun.

— esther & jerry hicks

i allow my actions to be infused with laughter
and joy. i live my life to the fullest, never taking
any moment too seriously, and i am
blessed with an amazing life.

i release all fears and doubts.

— louise l. hay

i release myself from fear and doubt.
fears and doubts are nothing but stumbling
blocks. i am strong, with limitless possibility.

i am flexible.

— deepak chopra

i am bendable and pliable and flow
freely with all that the universe offers.

my life works beautifully.

— louise l. hay

i am content to flow with the vibration
of life, and the universe provides justly for me.
i am rewarded with a beautiful life.

i do not make assumptions.

— don miguel ruiz

i am powerful when dealing with situations
and base all my decisions on fact, honesty and
integrity. i do not assume, but make choices
after consideration of all facts.

every thought i think
is creating my future.

— louise l. hay

every action i take comes from a positive
and empowering thought. i encourage others
to believe in me while empowering others
to believe in themselves.

i feel no guilt when
i say no to someone.

— brian l. weiss, m.d.

i create daily and choose powerfully the
way i live my life. everything i do is done for the
higher good for myself and for others. i trust in
my judgment and in the decisions i make.

i release the need for
struggle and suffering.

— louise l. hay

i deserve every happiness, and i create my
life free of hardship and suffering. i am truly
blessed. i stand tall and proud of who i am
and all that i have and will achieve.

i am surrounded by love
and light everywhere.

— miranda kerr

wherever there are shadows, there is always
a source of light. i cherish the light and love
that constantly surround me.

i am flexible and flowing.

— louise l. hay

i welcome each moment as it comes,
and life opens up in wonderful and exciting ways.
my experience of life is an adventure, and
i flow freely with it.

my life is too short not to do what i love.

— robert holden

my life is what i make it out to be.
i am present and living in the moment, and
anything i want for my life is waiting for me.
i love what i do and i do what i love.

i release all criticism.

— louise l. hay

i appreciate and accept that everyone is
entitled to their own opinion. criticism is just
that: nothing more, nothing less. i choose
powerfully and with love how or whether i react.

my mind is tranquil.
i allow peace into my life.

— leon nacson

i am at peace with my world, and tranquility
surrounds me as i bask in the glory of my life.

when i decide to be happy,
i attract great things in my life.

— robert holden

i have a beautiful life filled with happiness
and love, and i am rewarded with all the joy life
can offer. i naturally attract great things in my
life. everything i have, i have created.

there is plenty for everyone, including me.

— louise l. hay

life supports me in its abundance, and
the universe provides for me. i create my
life living powerfully in the present,
and appreciate all that i have.

i take the win-win approach.

— stephen r. covey

life abundantly provides for all. as i open
my heart and soul and share my opportunities
and rewards, the universe provides even greater
opportunities for me and others.

i love and approve of myself.

— louise l. hay

i am secure in my own skin and love myself
unconditionally. i approve of myself,
accepting my own individuality.

*there is nothing about my age
that prohibits me fulfilling my dreams.*

— dr. wayne w. dyer

my dreams are important to me right now.
my imagination and power are limitless.
nothing can stop me from achieving my dreams.

i accept my uniqueness.

— louise l. hay

i love and appreciate my own individuality
and uniqueness. i do not compare myself
with anyone or anything, as i am
confident in who i am.

i am patient.

— deepak chopra

i am patient, loving, and kind.
i know that i am in the right place at the
right time and the universe will provide.

*i am a vibrant, healthy, and
joyful being of light and love.*

— miranda kerr

every cell in my body radiates
love, health, and joy.

it is okay to be lonely now and then.

— louise l. hay

i take time out to be alone. i reflect on what is important and what i want for my life. i take time to nurture my soul, and i'm at peace with myself.

i have faith in my ability
to manifest my desires.

— deepak chopra

i manifest my dreams and desires daily, and have
faith in my abilities to achieve my dreams.

i now create a wonderful job.

— louise l. hay

i create my world, and i am receptive to
new opportunities. i am gifted, talented, and
grateful as i embark on the adventure
of creating my life daily.

i make and keep commitments.

— stephen r. covey

i honor my word and the commitments
i make to myself and to others.

loving others is easy when
i love and accept myself.

— louise l. hay

my love flows freely to others as i allow myself to
love, respect, appreciate, and accept myself.

everything i lose is found again;
everything that is hurt is healed again.

— caroline myss

everything in my world happens as it is meant
to happen. each change or experience
teaches me to grow and leads me to the
path i am meant to take.

i express my creativity.

— louise l. hay

i am creative. i express my creativity by allowing
my imagination, talents, and abilities to flow.
my creativity is a true expression of who i am.

i live a harmonious life.

— miranda kerr

i have an incredible family, great friends,
sweet pleasures, abundance, and wisdom;
i lead a harmonious life.

*i am open and receptive to
new avenues of income.*

— louise l. hay

i have no limits; i am limited only by my imagination. i am grateful, capable, open, abundant, and blessed. i embrace life's challenges and see them as opportunities.

every day i am a new person.

— brian l. weiss, m.d.

each day i create the life i desire.
i am free of any limiting past beliefs as
i reach for the stars and create my life.

i make healthy choices.

— louise l. hay

my body works tirelessly to protect me. i
nourish it by making healthy choices, and i
support it with the goodness, love, and
respect it deserves.

i am grateful for all that i have in life.

— deepak chopra

i am gratitude, abundance, and love.
i cherish my life and i am truly blessed.
all that i have and all that i am comes
from the power of being grateful.

whatever happens,
i know i can handle it.

— louise l. hay

i trust in my body's innate wisdom, and
i trust in the universe. i follow my intuition,
and i know that nothing is put before
me that i cannot handle.

i enjoy the friendship
and companionship of others.

— leon nacson

i welcome new friends and reinforce existing
relationships. i find time to consider the needs
and dreams of others and share in their joy.

*i know that blaming others does
not solve anything.*

— louise l. hay

i take responsibility for everything
i have created in my life. i do not blame others
for past mistakes. i am the creator of my
life and my experiences.

i will love where
i am right now.

— esther & jerry hicks

i am in the perfect space where i am meant
to be right now. i trust in the universe.
all that is meant to be will be.

i have friends i can talk to.

— louise l. hay

i express myself fully and openly with
my friends. i support them and they support
me, as we grow in our friendship and
experience all that life offers us.

everything i am searching
for is within me.

— miranda kerr

in being love, i give love;
in being joy, i give joy;
in being happiness, i give happiness.
everything i need is within.

i do not have to be a slave to
makeup or the latest fads.
i can just be myself.

— louise l. hay

i am perfect in all that i am and all that i am not.
nothing external to me determines my self-worth.
i am happy and content in being me.

i love and honor my creativity.

— deepak chopra

i am a creative human being with unlimited
and unrestricted potential. i love my creativity
and share it freely with the world.

i surpass other people's opinions of me.

— louise l. hay

i live my life knowing that who i am is an amazing
human being with unlimited potential. i do not
need the approval of others. i approve of, love,
and respect myself, and i am proud to be me.

whatever i can imagine,
the universe can deliver.

— esther & jerry hicks

i trust in the universe and know that i am
limited only by my imagination. i create the
space for my life to appear in, and the
universe delivers all that i ask for.

i conduct myself honorably at all times.

— louise l. hay

i am a loving, honorable, and compassionate human being. i treat others as i deserve to be treated: with honor, respect, and decency.

wellness is my natural state.
disease is an imposter.

— caroline myss

my heart and soul are nourished, my mind is
focused and active, and my spirit soars as
i bask in the wellness of my being.
i am healthy, happy, and content.

i am happy with my weight.

— louise l. hay

i nourish my body and accept that i am a totally unique human being—no one else is exactly the same as me. i am happy with who i am.

i demonstrate love through my actions.

— miranda kerr

everything i do is without malice or judgment.
i show my love through my actions and
through words of compassion.

it is okay to be sad sometimes.

— louise l. hay

everything in my world, good and bad,
creates who i am. i allow myself to experience
all emotions. for example, sadness grants me the
opportunity to fully appreciate all that i have.

i am free to create success
in my life—it is my choice.

— deepak chopra

i create my success daily—every decision and
every choice i make impacts the world. i live my
life to the fullest, knowing that i am the best that
i can be, and i am justly rewarded with
the success i choose.

i respect other people's boundaries.

— louise l. hay

i acknowledge each human being's uniqueness. i
respect other people's choices, and in turn
my choices are respected. i develop healthy
relationships based on mutual respect,
honesty, and understanding.

i am immune to others' opinions.

— don miguel ruiz

i am my own person, capable of making my
own decisions and choosing powerfully how i live.
i appreciate and respect what others have to say,
but ultimately i choose how i live my life.

i am grateful for each day.

— louise l. hay

i am grateful for who i am and who i am not.
i am grateful for the life i have been given and for
all that i have and all that i do not. every breath
i take is a blessing and an opportunity to fully
experience the sheer joy of being alive.

my life has meaning and purpose.
— deepak chopra

i am alive, vibrant, and focused. i make a difference in this world. my life has meaning and purpose, and i love all that life offers me.

i care about mother earth.

— louise l. hay

the universe provides for my every need.
i respect and honor our planet as
i bask in the glory of nature.

*i feel passionately about my life,
and this passion fills me with
excitement and energy.*

— dr. wayne w. dyer

life thrills me. i am passionate
about my goals and excited by the
opportunities the universe provides.

my happiness is an inside job.

— louise l. hay

i am content and happy. i love and appreciate
all that i have and all that i am. i choose my
happiness daily, and i am at peace with
myself and my world.

i feel compassion toward
myself and others.

— miranda kerr

i am a compassionate, loving, and gifted
human being. i live my life being the best i can
be and making a difference where possible.

i maintain a positive attitude.

— louise l. hay

i breathe positivity into my life with every breath i take. i see every experience, good and bad, as an opportunity to grow and expand my existence. i choose powerfully how i react, and i react powerfully to all that life offers me.

nothing is random or pure chance.

— deepak chopra

i am the creator of my life. nothing happens by chance. every thought, every action, has a reaction. i choose my words and my thoughts carefully, as they create my world.

i trust life.

— louise l. hay

i flow freely as the rhythm of life unfolds before me. i trust in the universal laws that create my experience daily and know that i am blessed.

the world is full of people
who would love to assist me.

— dr. wayne w. dyer

i ask for and accept an outstretched hand.
a time will come when i will give back to others
the goodness and love that has been given to me.

each day is a new opportunity.

— louise l. hay

every day brings new opportunities and
experiences. all i have is now, and
i choose to live life fully today.
i am vibrant, enthusiastic, and alive.

i am proud to be a woman.

— miranda kerr

i am a sensual, nurturing, and compassionate
woman. i am a woman of my word,
and i love who i am.

my family totally supports
me in fulfilling my dreams.

— louise l. hay

i am supported, loved, and appreciated.
my family supports me in achieving my dreams.

being myself involves no risks.
it is my ultimate truth,
and i live it fearlessly.

— dr. wayne w. dyer

i am fearless in my resolve to live my life
being nothing but me. i am real, authentic,
and true. i am my ultimate truth.

i listen to my body.

— louise l. hay

my body is made up of trillions of cells working in
unison to safeguard me. i appreciate my body and
take time out to nourish, rest, and
listen intently to its needs.

my outlook on life is unlimited.

— deepak chopra

i have no limits—i am limitless. i decide what
i want from life, and everything i want is available
to me. i believe in me and magic happens.

i love to exercise.

— louise l. hay

my body is unique. i listen to it and
honor it by taking time out to exercise.
i respect myself and empower my
mind by doing things that i love.

i love writing the script of my life.

— miranda kerr

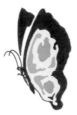

with passion and dedication, i create my life daily. with the pen poised, at every given moment, i write the exciting, miraculous script that is my life.

all is well in my world.

— louise l. hay

i trust that whatever happens to me,
happens for my highest good. every breath
i take creates my world—a world
i appreciate and cherish.

i compliment and praise others,
which enriches both of our lives.

— deepak chopra

i take time to acknowledge people for the gifts
they are in my life. i recognize and appreciate
the love that enriches my soul.

i am surrounded by loving, helpful people.

— louise l. hay

every human interaction brings a lesson
to my life, for which i am eternally grateful.
i acknowledge and appreciate everyone who
crosses my path, as all will teach me something.

it is never too late to create a new body.

— caroline myss

i am an incredible human being. every day,
by my thoughts and feelings, i create who i am
for myself. i create "me" today and tomorrow, and
i am happy with my creation. i am whole,
complete, and perfect just as i am

it is okay to ask for help.

— louise l. hay

i willingly receive the love and support of others.
i allow myself to trust and to be vulnerable, and
accept that i do not have to do it all on my own.

*i recognize and express
my unique talents.*

— deepak chopra

i am blessed to have unique and amazing talents.
i share the richness of these gifts with my family,
  friends, and society and hope it will benefit all.

i am willing to learn new things.

— louise l. hay

i am willing to learn and grow in each
new experience that life offers me.
there is a lesson in everything,
for which i am grateful.

a shift happens when i let go.

— robert holden

holding on to past situations inhibits my growth.
i choose to let go of past hurts. each day is a new
beginning and an opportunity to grow.

i am my own best friend.

— louise l. hay

i approve of who i am, what i stand for,
and what i believe in. i love being me,
and my own best friend.

i am excited and stimulated to act.

— leon nacson

as i wake, i breathe in the opportunity of each
new day, and i am grateful for the energy i have.
i am enlivened by life itself.

i stop and smell the flowers today.

— louise l. hay

i take time out to do the things in life that
i want to do. i surround myself in the glory of
nature. i am at peace with myself and the world.

*i have realistic expectations of others, and
they deal with me in the same way.*

— deepak chopra

i live in the world of appreciation,
not expectation, and my relationships
are harmonious and loving.

i am happy, calm, and peaceful inside.

— louise l. hay

i choose how i feel inside and how i react
at all times. i am worthy of anything i ask for
from life. i believe in me. i do not let negativity
get to me; i am happy, calm, and peaceful inside.

i release ill feelings toward
others without seeking retribution.

— leon nacson

i am forgiveness and love, and i move
forward knowing that the past does not impact
me or my future. every negative feeling i have
had is removed and replaced by
acceptance and love.

my income is constantly increasing.

— louise l. hay

the universe provides me with everything i need.
i am welcoming and open to all possibilities
and opportunities it provides. as a result,
i am prosperous and abundant.

every relationship teaches me something
valuable about myself and others.

— deepak chopra

i am open to continually learning new
things, being contributed to, and contributing to
others. every relationship i forge grants me
an opportunity to learn new things
about myself and others.

i trust my future to be positive.

— louise l. hay

i create my future daily,
filled with positivity and love.

i am sensitive to the thoughts
and feelings of others.

— deepak chopra

i communicate my feelings freely with those
i love, and i am sensitive to the thoughts,
needs, and feelings of others.

i appreciate everything in my life.

— louise l. hay

the universe provides me with incredible opportunities for which i am grateful. i take time out to appreciate my family and friends, and my life is filled with contentment and happiness.

i release all anger because anger harms me.

— brian l. weiss, m.d.

i allow myself to experience anger when it arises.
i acknowledge it, then release it from
my being so that i am free.

my healing is already in progress.

— louise l. hay

my body is a miracle. i visualize
love flowing from my heart, washing and
cleansing my mind, body, soul, and spirit.
i am healthy and full of energy.

my life is full of possibilities.
— deepak chopra

i walk through the door of opportunity, knowing
that anything i want for my life is possible and
i am worthy of anything for which i ask.

i am surrounded by love. all is well.

— louise l. hay

i am protected and safe, as i am completely
surrounded by love. my life is amazing.

i practice empathic listening.

— stephen r. covey

i practice love, compassion, and
understanding and am empathetic to the
needs of all living things. i listen and engage
in the lives of those around me.

it is safe for me to
speak up for myself.

— louise l. hay

my thoughts and opinions matter to me and to
others. i say what needs to be said, as i am strong,
confident, and just. i speak the truth always.

i speak with integrity.

— don miguel ruiz

i speak highly of others at all times, and
my word has integrity and strength. i do not
condemn, criticize, or complain, but instead
speak from the basis of truth and love.

my talents are in demand.

— louise l. hay

i am talented, courageous, and gifted ,and
my skills are in demand. the universe provides
me with ample time and opportunities
to achieve my dreams.

i intend to create good luck in my life.

— deepak chopra

i create every opportunity that
comes into my life. every breath, thought,
and action i take creates my world.

my circumstances at home
improve every day.

— louise l. hay

my home is my sanctuary—a sanctuary
i love to share with others. i create a peaceful
and loving environment for all, and relish
in the energy and love that flows from
the space i have created.

i choose nutritious food,
and treasure my body.

— miranda kerr

i am a unique human being. i treasure
my body and my mind, and i look after them
nutritiously so that they support me in my quest
to lead a fulfilled, fun-loving, and abundant life.

*my point of power is always
in the present moment.*

— louise l. hay

i choose powerfully to live in the present, not
concerned with the past or trying to predict the
future. i am powerfully present to the
abundance life offers me now.

life always gets better
when i treat myself better.

— robert holden

i deserve the best in this world, and
i treat myself with the respect and love
i willingly give to others.

i am the perfect age right now.
— louise l. hay

i am in the moment and enjoying every step of the way. i choose to live my life now, in every breath i take and in every moment.

*i have the ability to accomplish any task
i set my mind to with ease and comfort.*

— dr. wayne w. dyer

i have the ability and talent to achieve my
dreams, and i do so with gratitude, ease, and
grace, knowing all things are possible.

i release the past and forgive everyone.

— louise l. hay

i let go of any wrongs done to me or that i have done to others. i forgive myself and others, and i live in the present moment, allowing myself to relish new and exciting opportunities.

i came here to be me.

— robert holden

i give myself permission to be authentic.
i am fully self-expressed and never
afraid to be who i really am.

i am in the process
of positive change.

— louise l. hay

i am continually growing and learning, and
i create my future in every moment. my life
is exciting and full of limitless potential.

i refuse to eat emotional poison.

— don miguel ruiz

i am content. i approve and am at peace
with myself. my heart is true, and i am strong
in the face of any criticism.

i forgive myself.

— louise l. hay

i forgive myself, and i leave behind any
feelings of not being good enough.
i move forward freely with acceptance
and peace, knowing i did my best.

*i no longer worry about
the opinions of others.*

— brian l. weiss, m.d.

i listen to the opinions or advice of others, but
then i choose if it is right for me. every choice is
made knowing it is right for me.

it is okay for me to feel my feelings.

— louise l. hay

i allow myself to experience all my feelings.
as i release emotions, i give myself permission
to be with whatever thoughts and feelings arise
within me. i deal powerfully and justly
with all circumstances in my life.

i can heal anything by
healing my beliefs first.

— dr. wayne w. dyer

i believe in myself and my abilities.
i have unlimited potential when
i trust in the universe and believe in me.

i remember to tell my parents
how much i love them.

— louise l. hay

i always make the effort to tell my my mom
and dad how much i love them. i remind
myself that they need just as much love and
expressions of appreciation as i do.

i am committed to my goals.
i embrace uncertainty.

— leon nacson

whenever i'm surrounded by obstacles and
challenges, i know that if i arise above the
drama, answers will arrive and the
way forward will be clear.

my partner is the love of my life.

— louise l. hay

i am in a loving, intimate relationship
with a person who loves me for who i am.
we give and receive unconditional love
and our relationship is wonderful.

ACKNOWLEDGMENTS

There are many people who have made this book possible . . .

I would like to thank and acknowledge everyone at Hay House, especially Verusha Singh, Amanda Samson, Lisa Lord, Christine Dominguez, Dwayne Labbe, Rhett Nacson, and Leon Nacson for all their hard work and tireless dedication in publishing this book.

I also would like to thank Louise L. Hay, Deepak Chopra, Eckhart Tolle, Gurumayi Chidvilasananda, Yogi Bhajan, Daisaku Ikeda, and many of the other amazing spiritual teachers for their guidance and direction.

Marija Skara, Carlii Lyon, Tammy McCormack, Ian Mussman, Brandi Bennit, and Chris Colls, thank you so much for your endless support and patience.

To all the women who have contributed to my book by way of illustrating a flower, thank you, not only for your flower but for the contribution you have made to my life.

To my family especially my dad, mum, and brother Matt. Thank you for giving me the privilege of a loving, nurturing upbringing— you taught me the importance of family and I feel so blessed. To my whole family, including my nan and pa, aunts, uncles, and cousins, thank you for being the amazing people you are.

To my husband. Your wisdom and integrity constantly inspires me. Thank you for your unconditional love, acceptance, and understanding. And for touching my life in the most magical way.

To all who read this book . . . thank you for allowing me to share an incredible journey with you.

Lots of Love,
Miranda xxx

MIRANDA'S NETWORK

KORA Organic Skincare: Miranda has personally created her own skin-care line, KORA, in conjunction with a team of organic skin-care experts. It's a line that she loves and uses every day. The quality of the ingredients is KORA's number-one priority.

Miranda knows the success of her career is dependent upon her skin looking at its best, and in her remaining confident in her varying roles as one of the world's most sought-after supermodels.

KORA provides that confidence, and it is the company's goal to inspire women of all ages to follow Miranda's lead to nurture their bodies, embrace their unique beauty, and understand the benefits of organic skin care.

KORA contains pure essential oils and plant-derived and certified organic ingredients, and is enhanced by containing everything Miranda ever wanted in skin care for herself—all her knowledge of the tried-and-true beauty secrets are contained in the KORA line.

Miranda and KORA collectively strive to make a real and positive difference to people's skin.

"I have purposely added positive, loving words to every KORA skin-care product. Words like love, peace, empathy, and happiness, so that these positive vibrations flow through to the products and on to the person using them."

KORA products are available online from:
www.koraskincare.com, or by phone on 02 9979 5672, and from all David Jones retail stores across Australia.

Victoria's Secret: Miranda became a Victoria's Secret Angel in 2008 after working with the company for several years. She regularly travels to exotic locations around the globe with the Victoria's Secret crew, whom she regards as her adopted American family.

"Victoria's Secret is an amazing company. They really do treat all their people like Angels. It is a pleasure to work with such an inspirational company."

For further information on Victoria's Secret go to:
www.victoriassecret.com.

David Jones: Miranda has been the Fashion Ambassador for Australia's leading department store, David Jones, since 2007. She works with the store and leading designers to support and promote Australian fashion. She flies home to Australia several times a year to honor commitments including fashion, fun, racing, and in-store activities. Miranda also travels with the David Jones crew several times a year to shoot various campaigns for the retailer.

"David Jones is my other Australian family, and I am so proud to be associated with such an amazing company."

Chic Management: Miranda has been contracted to Chic Management (Australia) since she started modeling in Sydney in 2001. Prior to that she was with June Dally Watkins in Brisbane for her high school years. She particularly acknowledges Danielle Ragenard and Ursula Hufnagl for playing an integral role in the guidance of her career in Australia and overseas.

"I am blessed to have an agency that understands the dynamics of the industry so well. Chic has guided my career, and Ursula and Danielle are not only a large part of my management team in Australia, but also my dear friends."

Contact Chic Management at:

www.chicmanagement.com.au.

IMG Global: A team of professionals at IMG New York and around the globe sifts daily through available opportunities and offers Miranda guidance to ensure the continuing success of her international modeling career. Miranda particularly acknowledges her personal manager, Maja Chiesi, who has worked (even through two pregnancies and births) to guarantee that she achieves everything she desires on the international modeling front.

"What can I say? Thank you seems inadequate. IMG is an incredible global agency and I respect and value the people with whom I work so closely. Maja is my rock, she has become like a big sister to me, and I truly respect her and IMG."

See more about IMG at: www.imgmodels.com.

Miranda's Charities

The Koala Foundation: www.koalafoundation.org.au

Kids Helpline: www.kidshelp.com.au

About Miranda

Photo by Chris Colls

Miranda Kerr was raised on a farm in Gunnedah, Australia. Her first introduction to modeling came after winning the *Dolly/Impulse* modeling competition at age 14. Miranda completed high school and went on to study nutrition and health psychology at the Academy of Natural Living before deciding to model full-time.

Today Miranda is considered one of the world's top-earning models and a positive icon for young women. Her decade-long career has consisted of high-profile runway shows and fashion and beauty shoots, as well as advertising in television and print. She is a Victoria's Secret Angel and has appeared on the covers of numerous magazines, including *Vogue, Harper's Bazaar, Rolling Stone,* and *ID.*

In 2009 Miranda developed KORA Organics, a line of organic skin care made in Australia. Her aim was to inspire women globally to nurture their bodies, embrace their unique beauty, and understand the benefit of using organic skin care. The entire line is available at **www.koraorganics.com** and shipped all over the world.

Miranda has also loaned her time and image to charities and cause-related projects around the world, such as Kids Helpline Australia, the Art of Peace Charitable Trust, Cancer Council, the Breast Cancer Foundation, the Australian Koala Foundation, and Children International. She shares her life with her husband and son.

Please visit: **www.mirandakerr.net**

We hope you enjoyed this Hay House book.
If you'd like to receive our online catalog featuring additional information
on Hay House books and products, or if you'd like to find out
more about the Hay Foundation, please contact:

Hay House, Inc., P.O. Box 5100, Carlsbad, CA 92018-5100
(760) 431-7695 or (800) 654-5126
(760) 431-6948 (fax) or (800) 650-5115 (fax)
www.hayhouse.com® • **www.hayfoundation.org**

~~~~~~~

Published and distributed in Australia by:
Hay House Australia Pty. Ltd., 18/36 Ralph St., Alexandria NSW 2015 •
Phone: 612-9669-4299 • *Fax:* 612-9669-4144 • www.hayhouse.com.au

Published and distributed in the United Kingdom by:
Hay House UK, Ltd., 292B Kensal Rd., London W10 5BE • *Phone:*
44-20-8962-1230 • *Fax:* 44-20-8962-1239 • www.hayhouse.co.uk

Published and distributed in the Republic of South Africa by:
Hay House SA (Pty), Ltd., P.O. Box 990, Witkoppen 2068 •
Phone/Fax: 27-11-467-8904 • www.hayhouse.co.za

Published in India by:
Hay House Publishers India, Muskaan Complex, Plot No. 3, B-2, Vas-
ant Kunj, New Delhi 110 070 • *Phone:* 91-11-4176-1620 • *Fax:* 91-11-
4176-1630 • www.hayhouse.co.in

Distributed in Canada by:
Raincoast, 9050 Shaughnessy St., Vancouver, B.C. V6P 6E5 •
Phone: (604) 323-7100 • *Fax:* (604) 323-2600 • www.raincoast.com

~~~~~~~

<u>Take Your Soul on a Vacation</u>

Visit www.HealYourLife.com® to regroup, recharge, and reconnect
with your own magnificence. Featuring blogs, mind-body-spirit
news, and life-changing wisdom from Louise Hay and friends.

Visit www.HealYourLife.com today!